Newark's Little Italy

M. GIORDANO
SANITARY
BAKERY

Newark's Little Italy

THE VANISHED FIRST WARD

MICHAEL IMMERSO

A copublication of RUTGERS UNIVERSITY PRESS, New Brunswick, New Jersey,
and THE NEWARK PUBLIC LIBRARY, Newark, New Jersey

Library of Congress Cataloging-in-Publication Data

Immerso, Michael, 1949–

Newark's Little Italy : the vanished first ward / Michael Immerso.

p. cm.

ISBN 0–8135–2417–2 (alk. paper)

1. Little Italy (Newark, N.J.)—History—Pictorial works. 2. Newark (N.J.)—History—Political works. 3. Italian Americans—New Jersey—Newark—History—Pictorial works. I. Title.

F144.N66L55 1997

974.9'32—dc21 97–5674

CIP

British Cataloging-in-Publication information available

Third printing, September 1997

Manufactured in the United States of America

Design by John Romer

For my parents,

Nettie and Mickey,

and for all past and present members

of our family and especially

Jerry Gale

Campione's band parades on Seventh Avenue in 1915 with the Sons of Italy.
(Photo: Robert Salvatore)

CONTENTS

FOREWORD

This is a biography of the life of a Newark, New Jersey, neighborhood. It is an example of community history at its best, made all the more extraordinary by the fact that its inhabitants had been scattered and its homes leveled by the well-meaning but thoroughly devastating "urban renewal" efforts of the 1950s. The dispersion of the First Warders literally spans the continent, but their remembrance remains strong and their loyalty undiminished.

Michael Immerso has been able to tap this far-flung community to recover both memories and artifacts. In the process, he has developed a lasting "archive" of this once-vibrant community that we are thankful to house at The Newark Public Library.

Specifically, this community biography draws on the rich photographic documentation created by the First Warders who, by their selection of subject matter, preserved that which they believed was truly important in their lives. These images help illustrate and interpret the history of this community for the first time. This work should serve as a model for any community wishing to celebrate and preserve its unique history.

It is an honor to be a part of a collaboration with Rutgers University Press that has led us to the production of this important volume.

ALEX BOYD
Director
The Newark Public Library

Tubello children photographed on Eighth Avenue, circa 1925.
(Photo: Mildred Avitable)

ACKNOWLEDGMENTS

I wish to acknowledge the help of the following individuals who were among the many interviewed for this book: Anthony Genuario, Angelo Bianchi, Anthony Coppola, Monsignor Joseph Granato, Peter Rodino, Mary Mauro, Annette M. Nelson, the Zarro Family, Flora Russo, Rose Santuoso, Ursula Elefante, Angela Fayeux, Neil Maria, Clo Celentano, Mary Averna, Mary Boyd Iannacone, Tony Suppa, Rose Di Vincenzo, Joe Onofrietto, Dolores Nicastro, Rose Marinello, Steve Giordano, Babe Tubello, Theresa Colamedici, Connie Gesualdo, Mary Genzone, Connie De Gennaro, Rita Masi, Mildred Ceceri, Rose De Rogatis, and the many loyal parishioners of Saint Lucy's Church who lent their support and encouragement. Their devotion to the parish and its traditions is admirably detailed in Constance Petrucelli Ferrante's doctoral thesis, *A Walk Through Time: A Symbolic Analysis of the Devotion to Saint Gerard Maiella,* from which I benefitted. I am in debt to Kenneth Rosa, who transcribed Peter Mattia's journal, Giovanni Pinto, publisher of *L'Italico* newspaper, who compiled a record of early Italian settlers in Newark, and Ace Alagna, publisher of the *Italian Tribune,* who lent his full support to the project.

I am also in debt to the authors of several manuscripts and published works that explore Newark's Italian immigrant past, notably Olindo Marzulli's *Gl'Italiani di Essex;* Charles Churchill's *The Italians of Newark: A Community Study; The Italians in Newark, 1890–1914* by Patricia Flock; and *The Italians of Newark, New Jersey* by Fred Ensign Miles.

I received invaluable research assistance from Charles Cummings and the staff at the New Jersey Division of the Newark Public Library, as well as the staff at the New Jersey Historical Society. I am grateful to the director, editors, and staff at Rutgers University Press, including Marlie Wasserman; Steve Maikowski, who reviewed the initial proposal; Tricia Politi, production coordinator; John Romer, who designed the book; and especially Marilyn Campbell and Brigitte Goldstein for their help in guiding the book to its successful conclusion. I would not have been able to assemble the photo collection without generous financial support from the New Jersey Historical Commission, the Newark Landmarks and Preservation Committee, the Benedetto Croce Society, the Nicholas Martini Foundation, and especially Lillian Nowicke.

I wish to thank Larry Gianettino who assisted in the selection and reproduction of the photographs; Linda Lobdell, Tony Morello, and Tony De Lorenzo who assisted in various ways; my parents and my family, without whom I could not have undertaken this project; and most especially, my partner Elizabeth Ainsley Campbell who provided wise and patient counsel when it was most needed and who labored with me in the preparation of the manuscript.

PREFACE

The photographs brought together in this book capture the history of a remarkable American neighborhood. Newark's "Old First Ward" was a quintessential urban community, the kind of ethnic enclave that enlivened many American cities during the first half of the twentieth century. To those who came to visit, it was Little Italy, Newark's colorful Italian quarter, famous for its feasts, its Italian specialty shops, and its restaurant row along Eighth Avenue. For those who grew up there, it was something else. It was a beloved neighborhood, "the Ward," the first home of countless Italian immigrant families.

The history of this Italian community spanned only some eight decades. But in its heyday everyone from Al Capone to Enrico Caruso, from Thomas Edison to Marlene Dietrich came to visit. Joe DiMaggio dined on Eighth Avenue. Richie "the Boot" Boiardo held court at the famous Vittorio Castle. Proud First Warders were able to boast, "We had it all." Then everything came to an abrupt end.

In 1953 the heart of the First Ward was selected for urban renewal; thousands of First Warders were displaced, their homes were leveled by the bulldozers, and the neighborhood never fully recovered. Forty years have passed since the neighborhood was uprooted. Yet even now, it has the power to stir the emotions of those who recall the "flight of angels" during the Feast of Saint Michael or the sound of Italian bagpipes wailing in the cold midnight air during the Christmas Eve processions.

Despite the neighborhood's colorful past, the story of the First Ward has never been

told. No attempt has ever been made to document the history of the neighborhood or to preserve a visual record of its life. This is particularly disturbing because so much of it has been obliterated by urban renewal and decades of urban decay. The lack of a visual record led me to undertake this book. At first I had planned a short history of my family only. Like many of my generation who have roots in this Newark neighborhood, I grew up with stories of the First Ward. Whenever my extended family gathered for Sunday dinner, the conversation inevitably turned to reminiscing about Garside Street. I heard tales of U Fumo, the sweet potato man, of Fatigado, the peddler, and a host of other First Ward characters. Then, as if on cue, my uncle would turn to me and, waving his finger, he'd say, "Put that in the book." "What book?" I'd ask. I hadn't been planning to write one. But as time passed, I discovered that I did want to record those familiar stories of the neighborhood that were so much a part of our family lore.

Subsequent visits to various libraries and archives yielded very little about the neighborhood that had been preserved. Moreover, I began to feel the pressure of time. If one wanted to create an archive, it would have to be done soon. It would require the participation of an aging "last generation" of First Warders, whose oral history of the neighborhood could give meaning to the images. I decided to try.

The Newark Public Library agreed to serve as repository for the photograph collection I planned to assemble. But I was by no means certain that First Warders would respond to the project. Their response proved overwhelming. When the Star-Ledger ran a feature article about the project, photographs and memorabilia from hundreds of former First Ward families from all across the United States began to pour in. I examined more than sixty thousand photographs and selected approximately five hundred for the library's permanent collection. Most were culled from photo albums, attic trunks, and shoe boxes. One hundred and eighty are included in this book. They reflect the evolution of the district from a small Italian enclave in the last decades of the previous century to a complex, thriving Italian-American neighborhood during the first half of the present century. In almost every photograph, we see First Warders posing with an unabashed air of pride in their neighborhood. Through these images, the old streets and tenements come alive again, teeming and timeless.

Italian Heartland of the First Ward

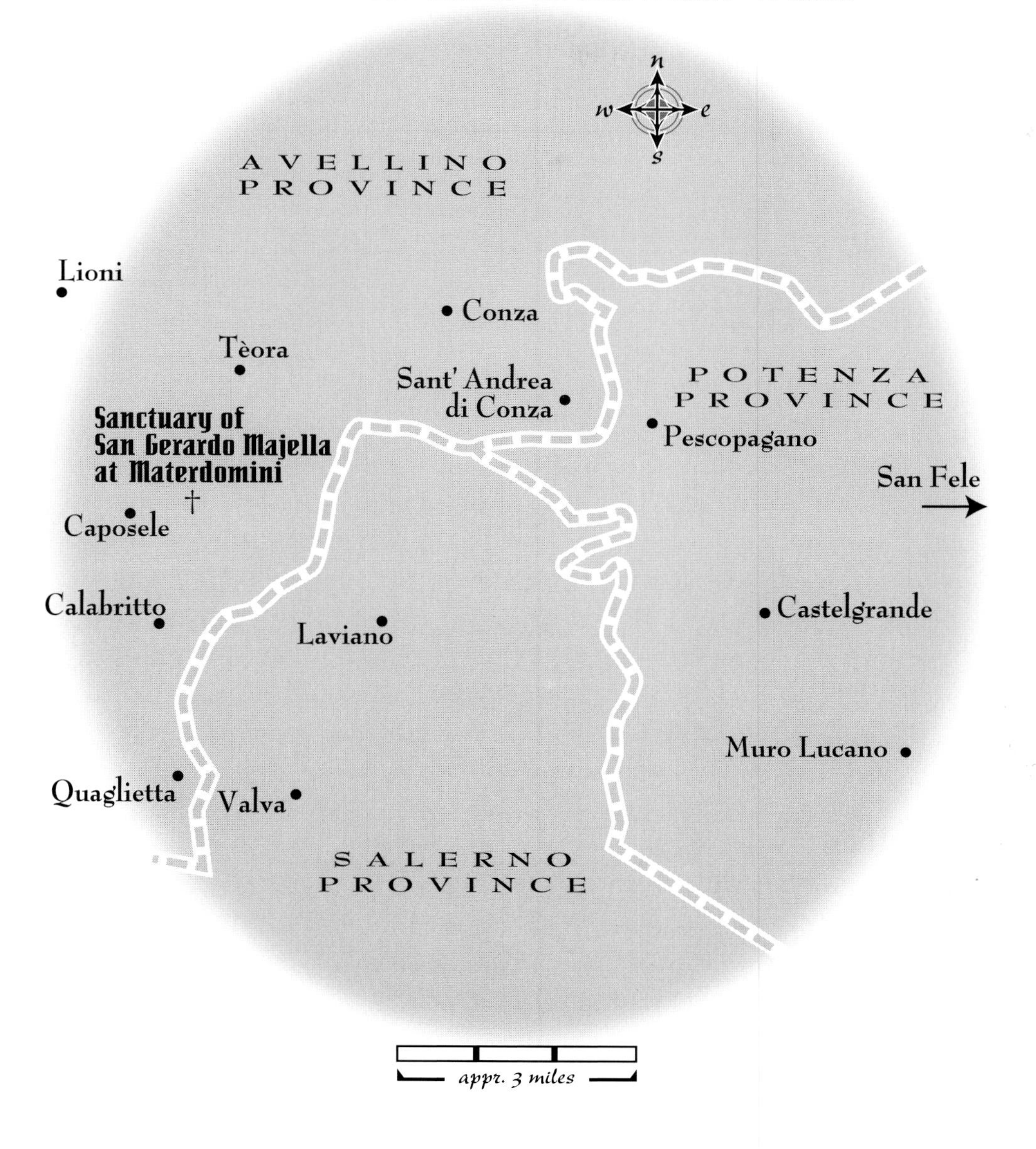

Wedding photo of Gerardo Cetrulo and Angelina Lisanti in Caposele, Italy, in 1901. Cetrulo was a renowned world fencing champion. Many of the early settlers of the First Ward, some depicted in this photo, came from Caposele. The Caposelese immigrants initiated the annual feast of Saint Gerard. (Photo: Dean Cetrulo)

INTRODUCTION

During the early stages of the southern Italian migration to the United States, the vast majority of those who came settled in New York City. Many settled first in New York's notorious Mulberry Bend district, and afterwards they established large enclaves in Italian Harlem, the South Village, Brooklyn, and the city's outer boroughs. Immigrants from southern Italy began settling in Newark, New Jersey's largest city, some eight miles west of Manhattan, as early as 1873. Newark thus became one of the first cities in the country outside of New York with a large Italian immigrant community. At the turn of the century, its Italian population ranked fifth in size nationwide, exceeded only by New York, Philadelphia, Chicago, and Boston. Newark's most densely populated "Little Italy" was concentrated in the First Ward.

When southern Italians began to arrive, Newark was a medium-sized city, a well-developed industrial and commercial center poised to embark on a period of rapid growth. The city's 105,509 residents (thirteenth in size of population in 1870) were almost entirely of English, German, Scottish, and Irish origin. Only twenty-nine Italians resided in the city then, all of them from northern Italy in the vicinity of Genoa, whose arrival a decade earlier preceded the great migration from the south.

Southern Italy in the later nineteenth century was afflicted with a series of

Families gather for a picnic in Caposele in 1913. Among them are members of the Russomanno, Malanga, Ceres, Chiaravallo, and Merola families who emigrated to Newark. (Photo: *Italian Tribune*)

economic setbacks and natural disasters which led millions to seek a better life overseas, particularly in the United States. A great many were peasant farmers from the small towns and villages in the Campania region that contains the city of Naples. It was a handful of immigrants from this region who established Newark's first southern Italian colony on Boyden Street, just north of the city's central business district, in what was then a largely undeveloped area that was part of the Eighth Ward and was later, until 1910, known as the Fifteenth Ward. This group of pioneers came from Avellino province in Campania, which was, together with several nearby provinces, to become the primary wellspring of the population of the First Ward.

The Italian heartland of the First Ward is a swath of land about fifty miles east of Naples where the Avellino, Salerno, and Potenza provinces meet. This rugged, mountainous territory is about fifteen miles wide and twelve miles deep, out of which flow the headwaters of the Sele River. Within it lie the towns of Teora, Caposele, Calabritto, Lioni, Conza, Muro Lucano, Castelgrande, and San Fele. From these villages and others nearby, such as Ricigliano, Atripalda, Monocalzati, Ariano Irpino, came a steady stream of people to the First Ward. Some came from Calabria, Apulia, and Sicily, but their numbers were much smaller.

The migration of southern Italians to Newark proceeded slowly at first, but was soon to gain momentum. In 1880 Italians residing in the city numbered 407. In the next three decades, between 1880 and 1910, approximately twenty thousand newcomers were added. By 1920, 27,465 Italians were living in Newark. They had established significant Italian enclaves in four distinct areas of the city. A large Italian quarter grew up in the East Ward, which is sometimes called the Ironbound district. A second Italian colony was established on Fourteenth Avenue and included many Sicilians. A third colony sprang up in the Silver Lake district at the northern edge of the city, spilling over into Belleville. The largest concentration of Italians, however, was to be found in the fourth colony, the First Ward.

The First Ward extended over an area of roughly 250 acres. It was bounded in the south by the tracks of the Lackawanna Railroad, in the west by Branch Brook Park, in the north by Bloomfield and Fourth avenues, and in the east by the Passaic River (to Clay Street) and Broad Street. In 1920 this area was home to 30,047 people. Italian-born residents numbered 8,109 and another 12,000 were the American-born offspring of Italian-born parents. Most resided in the crowded tenements that were clustered in the area around Saint Lucy's Church. The neighborhood also contained considerable numbers of Irish, Germans, Russians, Eastern Europeans, and African Americans. Although the percentage of Italians continued to increase over time, the First Ward remained culturally and racially mixed throughout its history.

Through most of its history, the First Ward evolved in a manner not unlike the Little Italys that sprang up in Philadelphia, Boston, Baltimore, and almost any other large American city. Boston's Italian North End, for example, like the First Ward, attracted growing numbers of Italians from Avellino province before the turn of the century and eventually became a district with a large concentration of Avellinese. The populations of both, Newark's First Ward and Boston's North End, expanded rapidly in the period before World War I, when the flood of immigration was at its peak. Both districts attained their highest population levels during the 1920s (the North End housed about 36,000 people on roughly 100 acres), and then both declined in density as Italians began to leave the crowded tenements in search of better living conditions. Nevertheless, both remained thriving Italian-American neighborhoods in the immediate postwar period.

In Newark everything changed in 1953, when urban renewal irrevocably altered the face of the First Ward. The district fell into a long period of decline and, today, hardly a vestige of the old Italian neighborhood remains. Nevertheless, its traditions and its memory are as alive and as potent today as they were more than four decades ago, the time when its residents were uprooted and displaced. These traditions are carried forward by a diaspora of former First Warders. The focus of this diaspora is the venerable Saint Lucy's Church, which still stands today. Every October, thousands come back to the old neighborhood for the annual Feast of Saint Gerard Maiella at Saint Lucy's Church. Many were born a generation or more after the neighborhood had ceased to exist. But they all share a special bond with a place and a past that are unrecoverable and yet very much alive. It is handed down to grandchildren and great-grandchildren who may never have directly experienced the vanished neighborhood, but who fiercely honor its memory.

Gabriello Valentino and his family pose with friends outside the family's bakeshop on Drift Street, circa 1890. (Photo: *Sunday Call* 3/25/1934)

"NEVARCA"

The founder of Newark's First Ward Italian colony was Angelo Maria Mattia, who settled on Boyden Street in 1873. Mattia was a woodcutter who came to New York City in 1872 with twenty-seven men from the town of Calabritto in Avellino province. The circumstances of his first visit to Newark are fancifully recorded in a journal kept by his son, Peter Mattia, who gave a firsthand account of the early southern Italian colonists in Newark. Mattia could not find work cutting wood and was too proud to work either as ditch digger (*zappatore*) or rag picker. He went to the docks in search of a job and by mistake boarded a ferry which carried him across the Hudson River. After wandering about for several hours, he encountered an Italian, one of a handful of Genoese living in Newark, who offered him a job at a Newark lumberyard. Mattia accepted and remained in Newark for one week. He then returned to New York and convinced his companions that there was plenty of work and space to live in "Nevarca." Mattia, who was sometimes called "Columbo" because he was first to arrive, settled on Boyden Street and with this small band from Calabritto, he established a colony of southern Italians that was to become the First Ward. There was a spare room in Mattia's house on Boyden Street, and for two years he provided free temporary shelter to able-bodied Italians who came in search of work or lodging.

They could stay for two weeks, whether they found work or not, but then had to move on to make room for new arrivals. Mattia could accommodate as many as ten boarders at a time. They slept on cots in an eighteen by ten foot common room. Some found work as day laborers, ditch diggers, factory hands, railroad men, or rag pickers, saving up enough money to send for their wives and families.

Slowly, at first, the Italian quarter in the vicinity of Boyden Street began to grow outward. In 1880 only 407 Italians were living in Newark, in small settlements on River and Bank Streets as well as Boyden Street. Italians occupied several buildings on Boyden Street and along Eighth Avenue. The building at 208 Eighth Avenue housed twenty-six Italians, including eleven children. These first Italian settlers worked at whatever trade they could. Antonio Cervone cut kindling wood. Donato Megaro fashioned jewelry. Vito Gerardo worked as a junk dealer. Census records suggest that a good number in the little Boyden Street colony were employed as rag peddlers, rag merchants, and peanut vendors.

Alfonso Ilaria's saloon at 31 Boyden Street became the focal point of the colony. Ilaria was among the first to settle on Boyden Street, having arrived in 1874. He was a colorful figure who was known as "King Alfonso." He was a stocky man with a dark complexion and a thick beard with a habit of brandishing a walking stick. His saloon, known as the Bee Hive, was a haven for Italians and a source of news. Ilaria was a man of many trades, a musician as well as a saloon keeper, who often acted as labor agent. He arranged the passage of workers from Italy and housed them in an Eighth Avenue boarding house he co-owned with a German woman.

The arrival of Italians on Boyden Street led to brawls with the Irish, who had long dominated Eighth Avenue in the vicinity of the Boyden Street quarter. To avoid conflicts, the Italians began to move west and north from Boyden Street toward Drift Street and Seventh Avenue. A few occupied a rookery on Drift Street. This sparsely settled area with very few dwellings had long been the city's quarry district. The undeveloped land included a large tract that later became Branch Brook Park. The area from Clifton Avenue to Factory Street, between Seventh and Eighth Avenue, consisted almost entirely of vacant land, except for a few buildings on Drift Street. The Essex County Brewery occupied the corner of Seventh Avenue and Clifton Avenue. The New Jersey Soldiers' Home (which housed Civil War veterans) occupied all of the land between Seventh and Sixth Avenue, from Mount Prospect Avenue to Wood Street. Italian laborers and masons cut and laid many of the streets and built and occupied almost every one of the buildings in this quarter. As their numbers increased, they eventually displaced the Irish on Eighth Avenue and on Boyden Street.

By 1886 as many as three thousand Italians were living in Newark and more were arriving every day. Italians were lured to Newark by the demand for labor in the mid-1880s when the Pennsylvania Railroad began laying tracks across the meadows connecting Jersey City and Newark. The Shanley Brothers, Newark contractors, had the task of supplying the labor for the railroad. They made use of Italian *padrones* to secure work gangs. The padrone acted as an agent who supplied the contractor with a steady pool of cheap Italian labor. Thousands of Italians labored on railroad gangs, earning as little as ninety-five cents for a day's work. Countless others worked as street laborers and ditch diggers. Beginning at about 1895, Italian laborers were employed in the laying out of Branch Brook Park. The Essex County Park Commission engaged the Olmsted Brothers to help design the park and employed padrones to hire Italian laborers. While the park was under construction, a padrone was murdered and subsequently a law was enacted in New Jersey abolishing the padrone system. Many Italian laborers were so-called "birds of passage" who came here to work part of the year, often boarding together, and then returned home. They made frequent trips back to southern Italy, taking with them news that many *paesani* from Avellino province had settled in Nevarca. As a result, many more Italians from Caposele and Teora, from Lioni and San Fele, left their homeland bound for Nevarca.

As the colony grew, Italians established their own businesses and gave the quarter their own special character. Alfonso Sibilia opened the first pastry shop on Sheffield Street. The first Italian spaghetti restaurant was on the corner of Factory Street near Eighth Avenue. Francesco Maulano established one of the first macaroni factories in New Jersey on Sheffield Street. He employed twenty people in its bakeshop and delivered its product to his customers with fifty-two horses and wagons. Some years later Francesco Chiaravallo began to manufacture macaroni with electric motor power in a small factory on the corner of Nassau and Sheffield Streets. Citywide, Italians soon asserted themselves as a respected presence in the community. The first Roman Catholic Italian parish, Saint Philip Neri's, was established in 1887 in the Italian quarter near the County Court House. In 1891, Columbia Hall, the first Italian meeting hall, opened on Market Street and became the headquarters of numerous Italian organizations in the city. The following year, thirty-two Italian societies took part in a celebration marking the four hundredth anniversary of Columbus' discovery of America. They marched down Broad Street and dedicated a plaque at City Hall.

The family of Michele Nittoli and Pasqualina Perna, circa 1900, shortly after they came to the First Ward from Lioni, Italy. (Photo: James Lecky)

The Adubato family on Thanksgiving Day 1908, in the backyard of Celesta Adubato's house on Eighth Avenue. She was among the first southern Italian settlers in Newark. Tom Adubato, who gained local fame as an heroic Italian police detective, is standing at far left. (Photo: Gerry Pesci)

Studio portrait of Alfonso Ilaria ("King Alfonso") with his wife Adelina. Ilaria was one of the first Italians to settle on Boyden Street. His sister, Filomena, was the wife of Angelo Mattia. When she came to America in 1874 to join her husband, Alfonso accompanied her to Newark. Alfonso Ilaria's Boyden Street saloon became the focal point of the Italian colony which eventually became the First Ward. (Photo: Arlene Milone)

Though the Italians form a very small part of the population of Newark, they are steadily growing in numbers and, as a rule, are quiet, inoffensive people, and many of them are industrious and thrifty and are steadily making money. There are about 1000 Italians in the city. . . . They come chiefly from Naples and a more ragged, dirty set of people it would be hard to imagine. They are, many of them, rag and bone pickers and some of them work on the street occasionally. . . . Others from the south are organ grinders, and these chiefly reside in Drift Street, Eighth Avenue, and River Street. They hire their organs in New York for the season, go about the streets playing upon them, and at night herd together in large numbers in one house. On Sundays, when these people cannot follow their usual occupations, many of the natives of South Italy follow the occupation of bootblacks.

SENTINEL OF FREEDOM
(5/31/1881)

Studio portrait of Raffaele and Rosina Tubello, circa 1890. They emigrated from Caserta and settled on Eighth Avenue. Raffaele worked as a baker, then as an iceman, and eventually established a coal and ice business. He died in 1915. Rosina ran the coal business until her death in 1933. (Photo: Tubello Family)

Family of George and Vittoria Mauro, photographed in 1916. The story of Vittoria Mauro, who came to Newark in 1910, is quite typical. Vittoria did not want to come to America. Her husband Giorgio worked in the salt mines in New York and although he made several return trips to Italy, Vittoria resisted. Giorgio threatened never to return to Italy if his wife would not join him in America. Vittoria finally agreed to come. She was seven months pregnant and during the voyage she was so ill she could only eat crushed ice. When the boat docked in New York, Vittoria felt too weak to walk until informed that she would have to return to Italy if she was unable to leave the ship. The thought of a return voyage was so terrible, Vittoria found the strength to disembark. She lived to be a hundred years old. (Photo: Mary Mauro)

The family of Joseph Linarducci, one of the first Italians elected to public office in New Jersey. He served as a member of the State Legislature.
(Photo: Margaret Linarducci)

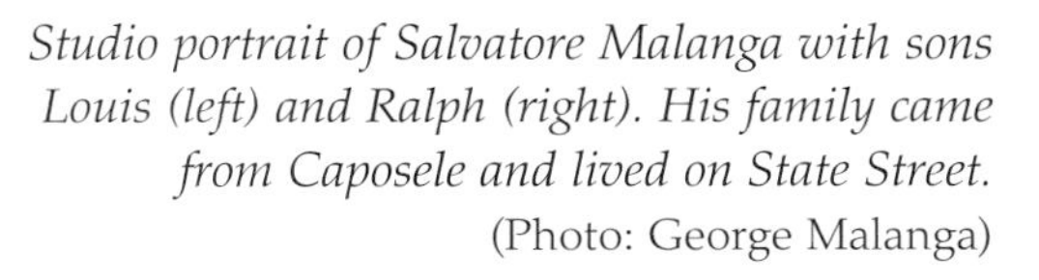

Studio portrait of Salvatore Malanga with sons Louis (left) and Ralph (right). His family came from Caposele and lived on State Street.
(Photo: George Malanga)

Italian laborers are coming to this city from their sunny native land in shoals. Every steamer that arrived in New York during the past three months brought a large number of these swarthy men. Newark has received a large percentage of these semi-nomads. Few of the Italians in this city beg from door to door. Like the Chinese they live upon food upon which others would starve . . . River Street is the headquarters of the Italian population and there are branch colonies on Adams, Boyden, and Drift Street and also on Seventh, Eighth, and Fourteenth Avenue, but they never live where the Germans reside in large numbers. They are clannish because they cannot speak English, and also because they do not know how to conform to American customs.

SUNDAY CALL 5/30/1885

Antonio Cuozzo and family on his wedding day in 1912. (Photo: Norma Cuozzo)

The family of Alfonso and Carmela Primamore, circa 1917.
They arrived from Italy in 1903 and lived on Webster Street. (Photo: Peter Primamore)

Family of Sabino Zarro and Maria (Zoppi) Zarro, circa 1926, with children Frank, Gennaro, Tom, and Marie. (Photo: Zarro Family)

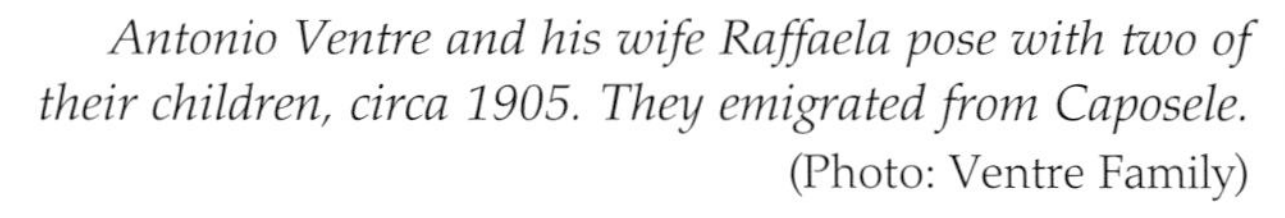

Antonio Ventre and his wife Raffaela pose with two of their children, circa 1905. They emigrated from Caposele. (Photo: Ventre Family)

> The Italian is here and he is here to stay. He is learning our language and our ways and it would be well for the police to discourage the habit that some boys have . . . of calling the Italian by any but pet names and annoying him generally. . . . The Italian by birth has a more impetuous nature or emotional turn of mind than a Chinaman, for instance, and his patience is liable to give out sooner.
>
> MAYOR JOSEPH E. HAYNES
> *Mayor's Annual Message, 1892*

Vincent Nicodemi (left) and Ralph Nicodemi (right) pose with a friend outside Nicodemi's Café. (Photo: Paul D'Ascensio)

LITTLE ITALY

At the turn of the century, Newark's Italian districts were undergoing great changes. The transformation of the Boyden Street colony was so striking in the first years of the new century that the newspaper *La Frusta* (The Whip) was able to boast in 1904, "Today it is the nicest quarter of the city." New buildings, erected by Italians, replaced old dilapidated, frame houses on Eighth Avenue, Drift Street, and Factory Street, and new cafés and restaurants appeared. A steady stream of new arrivals from Italy spurred the growth of the district, so that by 1910, Newark had the fifth largest Italian population in the country. About twenty-one thousand Italians were living in the city. Most had arrived in the previous three decades with practically empty pockets. Their heavy concentration in the area of the First Ward, known as Little Italy, added a boisterous, colorful atmosphere to that part of the city.

Eighth Avenue, the enclave's main thoroughfare, and Seventh Avenue, from Stone Street to Garside Street, were lined with pushcart peddlers, barkers, and vendors, calling out their wares, straining to be heard above the din of competing voices. Italian merchants operated scores of shops along these streets. A directory of Italian businesses compiled in 1911 counted sixty-three grocery stores, four macaroni manufactures, seventeen bakeries, twenty-three shoe repair shops, forty barbershops, and eighty-eight saloons.

Saloons, such as Masi Hall and Silvis Hall on Eighth Avenue, had meeting halls where musical performances were offered. Strolling Italian mandolin bands were a common sight along the avenue. Musicians performed in cafés, in barbershops, and on street corners. Bands, such as the Banda Nazionale, Federico Campione's Banda Bianco, and the Italian Royal Orchestra, played at feasts, funerals, parades, and social gatherings. Italian singers and novelty acts performed at the Columbia Vaudeville Theater on Seventh Avenue. The popular satirical singer Eduardo Miggliaccio, known as "Farfariello" (Little Butterfly), frequently performed there, and when he did the theater was always full.

American silent films were presented at the same theater as well as at the Vitale Brothers Theater on Seventh Avenue. During the showing of films, the theater manager, Gerardo Megaro, provided an Italian narration to accompany the action taking place on the screen. Price of admission for the movies was five cents. Large-scale musical productions, including Italian operas, were staged at the New Theater on Orange Street. A particularly popular form of entertainment was the traditional Italian marionette theater presented at the Teatro di Marionette on Seventh Avenue which staged elaborate productions with two feet tall puppets. Performances at the theater, which seated two hundred patrons, were always well attended.

Italian fraternal organizations and mutual aid (mutuo soccorso) societies proliferated in Newark's Italian neighborhoods. For each Italian hometown, represented in sufficient numbers, a mutual aid society was organized. The membership of these societies ranged from about forty to one hundred members (soci). They provided sick and death benefits for members while also functioning as a social outlet. Members paid about fifty or sixty cents monthly dues and everyone contributed about two dollars for death benefits when a member died. The treasury (*fonda cassa*) varied, from less than two hundred dollars to as much as fifteen hundred dollars. Large fraternal organizations, such as the Guards of Columbus, had about two hundred members. Meetings were held monthly. There were fifty-three Italian mutual aid societies in Newark in 1910. About thirty Italian fraternal organizations and mutual aid societies existed in the First Ward, including Societa Cavour, Societa Fraterno Amore, Societa Aviglianese, Societa San Sabino Atripaldese, Societa Garibaldini, Societa Calabrittana Arti e Mestieri, and the Societa 1.o Battaglione d'Africa, composed of Italian Army veterans of the 1886 Ethiopian campaign. Fraternal organizations and mutual aid societies catered to diverse needs within the emerging immigrant community. Those who had successfully established themselves and wished to assert their national heritage might join the Columbian Guards. Workingmen might choose to affiliate with a workmen's "protective association"—the Master Barbers Mutual Aid Protective Union, for example.

The vast majority of Italian heads of households were laborers and factory workers. Some were employed in nearby factories, such as the Westinghouse factory on Lackawanna Avenue and the Clark Thread Mill. An average Italian household at the time subsisted on an annual income of about six hundred dollars. Among the poorest Italian laborers were the men who worked with picks and shovels, cutting trenches, digging sewers and cellars, paving streets, and laying trolley lines. They worked a ten-hour day for wages of twelve to seventeen cents an hour, and sometimes less. In 1912, Italian laborers formed the Independent Laborers' and Diggers' Union and over two thousand men went on strike demanding an hourly wage of twenty-five cents and an eight-hour workday. During the six-week strike, the First Ward became the scene of a pitched battle along Seventh Avenue between the police and more than three thousand men, women, and children. A sixteen-year-old boy died during a subsequent clash. The situation for many strikers became desperate and their wives were said to be "begging at bakeries for loaves of bread." Food depots were set up on Cutler, Garside, and Drift Street, and leaders of the Italian community, such as Dr. Angelo Bianchi and Dr. Alfredo Magnani, the Italian consular agent, embraced the cause of the strikers. Although it failed to achieve its objectives, the strike brought the most destitute laborers into the fold of the organized labor movement and thus set the stage for gains in the future.

As the district grew, it was able to support a modest professional class. Among the newly arrived from Italy were men who established law offices, medical practices, banks, newspapers, and civic and fraternal associations. There were lawyers such as Ernesto and Gaetano Belfatto; doctors such as Panacrazio Megaro and Giuseppe Malatesta; bankers such as Salvatore D'Auria; and newspaper publishers such as Pasquale Matullo and Francesco Fiore. Several Italian language newspapers and journals, among them *La Montagna, La Frusta, La Ravista, L'Ora,* and *L'Avanti,* were published in the colony. And for the first time, Italians such Lorenzo Boscaino, Richard Mattia, and Dr. Angelo Bianchi, won election to public office. Politically, most Italian immigrants aligned themselves with the Republican Party.

The years leading up to World War I witnessed an Italian community grown confident and proud of its heritage. In September 1916, fifteen thousand Italians paraded through downtown Newark on the anniversary of the liberation of Rome. When the United States entered the war, as an ally of Italy, Italians enlisted in great numbers. Many considered it an opportunity to affirm their loyalty to their adopted land as well as a way of obtaining citizenship. Emotions ran so high that a riot erupted at McKinley School when a teacher made critical remarks about the Italian army. A large crowd descended on the school and the teacher had to be rescued by the police. So many young men enlisted that when the First

Ward displayed its service flag in 1918, it was decorated with a thousand stars. The flag, adorned with the national shields of Italy and the United States, was carried through the neighborhood, and hoisted aloft over Cutler Street. When word of the armistice finally came, the entire neighborhood erupted with joyous emotion. People wept in the street. They banged on pots and pans and paraded through the streets with torches, waving Italian and American flags. A Garside Street peddler rode in a hearse with an effigy of the defeated Kaiser, and the pastor of Saint Lucy's Church, the Reverend Joseph Perotti, rang the church bell for a full half hour.

Frank Biondi's butcher shop at the corner of Cutler Street and Sixth Avenue, circa 1917. The proprietor's wife Mary Muscarrilla Biondi, is at right. Her daughter, Mary Biondi Spera, is behind the counter. (Photo: Richard Yanuzzi)

Members of the De Lucca family (at right) pose outside their harness shop at 202 Eighth Avenue, circa 1915. (Photo: Dr. Frank Alfano)

Interior view of Cafe Roma at the corner of Seventh Avenue and Factory Street, circa 1906. Pictured are Jennie De Vito and her sons Americo, Eddie, and John. (Photo: John De Vito)

Bartenders Ralph Nicodemi (left) and Vincent Nicodemi (right) with their nephew, Gen Barone, at Nicodemi's Café at 100 Seventh Avenue. (Photo: Paul D'Ascensio)

Rizzero D'Ambola poses outside his store at 23 Factory Street in 1917. (Photo: Lena Montalbano)

Frank Alfano and his family at his store at 201 Eighth Avenue, circa 1915. (Photo: Dr. Frank Alfano)

No one in the First Ward commanded more respect than Doctor Bianchi. He would arrive at his patient's house in his horse and buggy, and if the family was too poor to pay, he would bring food. Bianchi established a private hospital on Summer Avenue—the first Italian institution of its kind in New Jersey—and later had a lasting association with Newark's Columbus Hospital. During his long career, he delivered more than 6,500 babies. Bianchi once encountered a city employee berating an Italian street sweeper outside Newark City Hall. As Bianchi approached, the man apologized, saying, "I meant no disrespect to you, Dr. Bianchi." "But you don't respect this poor fellow," Bianchi replied, vowing to have the man fired. When informed that only an alderman could do so, Bianchi decided to run for office. Italians overwhelmingly voted Republican, and Bianchi had to campaign as a Democrat to unseat the incumbent. "It's a pity the Democrats must sacrifice a fellow like you," a rival observed. Bianchi replied, "The Romans say a small pebble can halt an entire army." He won the election. When he later encountered his old rival, the man conceded, "Bianchi is a great boulder." Bianchi had several encounters with Thomas Edison. When they first met, Dr. Bianchi noticed that Edison had a rash on his hand. He wrote out a prescription and gave it to the famous inventor. Edison had already consulted several physicians, but nothing had worked. Bianchi swore this would cure him. Two weeks later Edison appeared at Bianchi's office on Seventh Avenue to thank him. The rash had disappeared. A short time later, Bianchi found himself with a sizable sum of money to invest and he sought Edison's advice. Edison arranged a meeting with a business partner and invited Bianchi to attend. When Bianchi arrived, Edison's friend greeted him with the remark, "I was astounded to learn someone of your race has such a large sum to invest." Bianchi refused to shake his hand. "I won't do business with you," he replied, and he abruptly left the meeting. The man was Henry Ford.

Dr. Angelo Bianchi, circa 1925.

Photo: Angelo Bianchi

Doctor Angelo Bianchi, seated at the far end of the table, during a dinner party in his honor at a First Ward saloon, circa 1918. (Photo: Angelo Bianchi)

Studio portrait of Maestro Federico Campione, circa 1920, with members of an Italian-American association. Campione was director of the Banda Bianca (White Band), which performed at feasts, parties, balls, picnics, and funerals. He advertised his services with a notice in local newspapers stating: "The Banda Bianca has a very fine repertory whether for orchestra or for marching band as well as most elegant new uniforms. All engagements must be made with Maestro Sg. Federico Campione." (Photo: Vito Del Vecchio)

Sabino Zarro, circa 1918, poses with his bootblack stand. (Photo: Diane Dunn)

Emidio Russomanno photographed inside his cobbler shop at 5 Boyden Street, circa 1920. (Photo: Florence McCoullough)

Guiseppe Antonio Basso in his barber shop at 83 Seventh Avenue, circa 1920.
(Photo credit Daniel P. Quinn)

Construction of Sacred Heart Cathedral, circa 1910. Italian stone masons, such as Luca Tobia (front row, third from left), came to Newark to work on the construction of the cathedral. This group of masons posed on the altar of the cathedral facing the unfinished rear chapel. (Photo: Phyllis Scanzillo; Robert D'Auria)

Columbian Guards Ball Committee of 1900. (Photo: *Sunday Call* 9/10/1933)

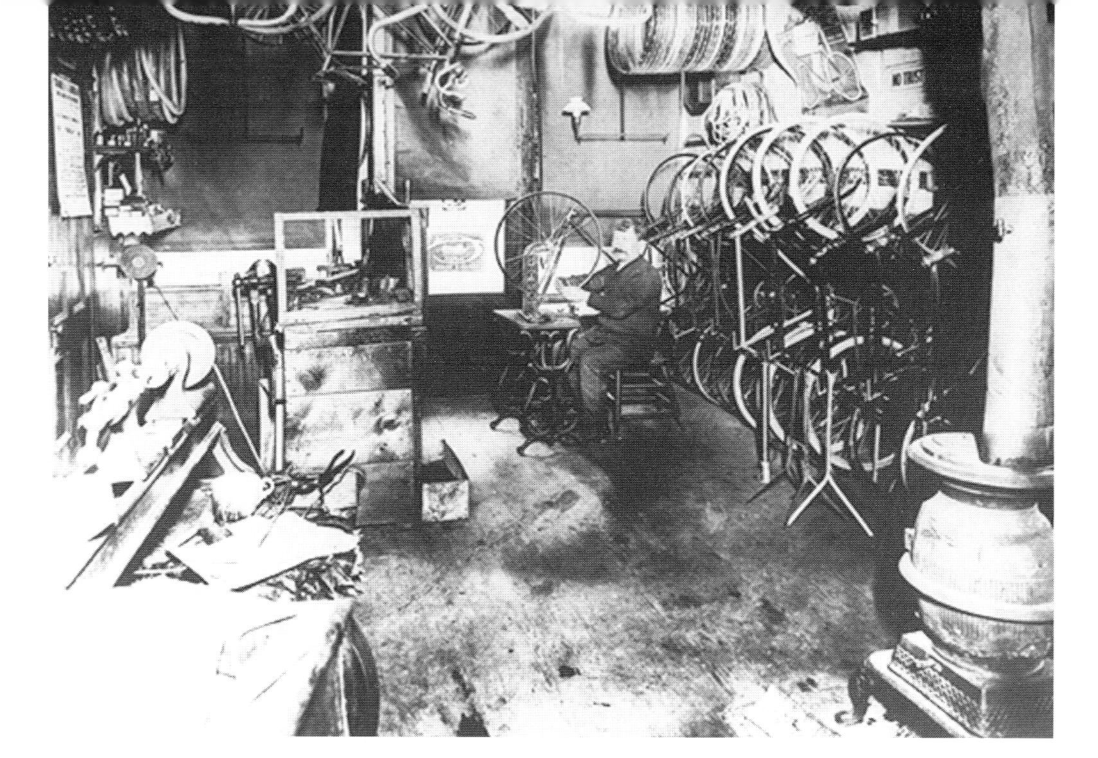

Vito Nole poses inside his lock and bicycle repair shop at 11 Summer Avenue, circa 1920. (Photo: Vito Nole)

Members of the Societa Fraterno Amore di Mutuo Soccorso fra Caposelesi (brotherhood of love) pose on Eighth Avenue near Nesbitt Street in 1924. The earliest Caposelese society, it was sometimes known as the Fratallanza. It was succeeded in 1935 by the Circolo Progressivo Caposele, which was originally a guild of tailors from the town of Caposele. Their patron, San Gerardo Maiella, had also been a tailor before entering the monastery. (Photo: Spatola Family; Rocco Freda)

Portrait of Andrea Masi, bandleader and proprietor of Masi Hall at 210 Eighth Avenue. Masi led a "parade band" which played at funerals and feasts. He was sometimes called the "Mayor of Eighth Avenue." (Photo: Rita Masi)

Domenico Valentino, a founder of the Columbian Guards, poses in his uniform, circa 1900. (Photo: *Sunday Call* 9/10/1933)

Portrait of Maria Zoppi, circa 1916, age seventeen. (Photo: Diane Dunn)

Street scene along Eighth Avenue in 1917. The building was owned by saloon keeper Michael Tuozzolo. (Photo: Rose Marinello)

Alfonso del Negro, a widower, photographed with his daughters Elvira, Elsie, and Madalene in 1912. They performed at various halls in the First Ward during the early 1900s. (Photo: *Italian Tribune*)

TEATRO DI MARIONETTE

The marionette playhouse in Seventh Avenue, in the heart of the Italian colony, is apparently a prosperous institution and the performances are well attended and the work performed upon the stage appreciated to an extent hardly conceivable unless one is thoroughly acquainted with the race.

To an American visitor, the audience is as much a part of the show as the stage performance, and it is as full of variety. Women rarely attend these presentations. Men and boys make up the house and they differ from the American audience just as the people differ in their racial traits.

While the play is in progress, the varying expressions on the features of the audience are a study. Every word spoken and every movement taking place in the unfolding of the drama is duplicated in the mobile countenances of the rapt auditors.

The marionettes are each a little over two feet high. They are so jointed that when they are held up by the manipulators by the strings and wires, they have the appearance of using their hands, feet and head in a very human fashion.

Swords clash and armor clanks and shields crash in a most realistic manner. The manipulators have to work hard behind the scenes during this great combat. Some of the figures weigh, with their armor, thirty or forty pounds each and it requires no small amount of skill to handle them all.

Sunday News 4/10/1904

Garside Street, circa 1912. The photograph is apparently the work of the photojournalist Jessie Tarbox Beals. (Photo: Newark Public Library)

GARSIDE STREET

The neighborhood's residents called the block between Seventh Avenue and Sixth Avenue "First Garside." In 1920 this single block on Garside Street housed 1,227 inhabitants. All but ten were Italian. Four hundred and forty-six were children below the age of ten. They were crowded into just thirty-one buildings, none higher than five stories.

First Garside, like other crowded neighborhood blocks, was a small community within the larger neighborhood. Salvatore D'Auria's Bank, at the corner of Seventh Avenue, dominated one end of the block. A small park occupied a corner at Sixth Avenue. In the days before Prohibition, this one block had nine saloons. The saloons and cafés, as some were called, gave a lively air to Garside Street. Racioppi's Saloon at 31 Garside Street was headquarters of the Teorese Society. It was a popular gathering place and some still recall the time when Enrico Caruso stopped by for a drink. The Tricolle Café at 43 Garside Street was a meeting hall for the Sons of Italy and other Italian organizations. The Star Hall Café had a dance hall and was a haunt for local musicians. During Prohibition, bootleggers stored barrels of illegal wine in the cellar of the Star Hall Café. When the Alcoholic Beverages Commission raided the place, the agents rolled the barrels into the street and broke them open with axes. Garside Street was flooded with wine and neighbors ran to get pots and pails to scoop it up.

Several Italian-language newspapers were published on Garside Street. The block also housed two bakeries, two funeral homes, two macaroni factories, a poultry market, two meat markets, two barbershops, and a coffee store. Two shoemakers, a tailor, a hatmaker, and a watchmaker also did business on the street.

In the daytime, both ends of Garside Street echoed with cries of "Guahl-yo!" as young boys called out to one another. On warm summer evenings children slept on the fire escapes, while the older folks sat on the stoops below and talked late into the night. Sometimes Nick Lucas, the famous "crooning troubadour" who is best remembered for his 1929 hit recording of "Tiptoe through the Tulips," would serenade with his guitar. At summer's end, children on Garside Street collected strawhats to display, like trophies, on the electrical poles. They gathered on the fire escapes armed with a string and a hook to capture the hats from the heads of willing gentlemen passing below. Election Day was celebrated with a bonfire on Garside Street. Crates, boxes, and refuse were collected days in advance of the cry "Go for elections!" and were then set ablaze in the middle of the street. The flames sometimes reached as high as the rooftops.

Garside Street, in those days, was populated by people who were by no means extraordinary but who, nonetheless, left a lasting impression on everyone who grew up there. Shopkeepers such as the butcher Ze Michele and a storytelling grocer called Ze Cunzalade enlivened the experience of daily life in ways that are difficult to measure but bring a smile to the faces of those who came from First Garside. The butcher Michele Blasco was known to everyone on Garside Street as "Ze Michele." His wife was a tiny woman called "Zia Cugatina." Ze Michele had a drum. Every year, when the neighborhood celebrated the Feast of Saint Gerard, he walked in the procession from early morning until late in the evening, beating his drum. When Ze Michele was asked what he played on his drum, the butcher replied, "Debito sopra debito, debito sopra debito," which means, "Debts upon debts, debts upon debts." Ze Michele often was called to a neighbor's house to repair an out-of-joint shoulder or twisted knee. He would appear at the door reeking of meat. Then, with hardly a word, he would crack the joint back into place. Ze Cunzalade's grocery store was at 7 Garside Street. The old man held a flank of prosciutto under his chin like a violin as he told stories of Italy and bandits and slowly sliced the meat with his knife while the children watched mesmerized, fearing a fatal slip of the blade at any moment.

Palagonia's Macaroni Store at 12 Garside Street was a typical, small Italian macaroni factory. In the front was a little grocery shop; in the back were various machines for making the pasta and sacks of flour piled almost to the ceiling. Palagonia hung his pasta to dry on poles in a storeroom behind the shop. He sold it uncut, wrapped in white paper. One often saw swarms of young boys going about Garside Street balancing the long strips of pasta in broad white bundles.

Faticado's fruit and vegetable stand was at 10 Garside Street. Faticado and his brothers were peddlers (faticare means to labor), and sometimes he let the children from the block ride on the back of his wagon in the empty vegetable crates. When he got rid of his wagon, he opened a little vegetable stand. Faticado had a glass eye. He slept half the day, and the children were often tempted to steal his apples. But because of that glass eye, which always peered open, they could never be certain that he was asleep.

D'Auria's Bank was at the corner of Seventh Avenue and Garside Street. Salvatore D'Auria was one of the most prosperous men on Garside Street. He arrived in Newark in 1885. At first he worked as a stonecutter. He saved his money and eventually opened a grocery store. In a few short years he owned his own bank. Like many Italian bankers, he began his business as a steamship ticket agent who held his neighbors' money for safekeeping. Operating a steamship agency could be very lucrative because Italians made frequent return trips to Italy or arranged for their families to come to this country, so rows of steerage trunks were often piled up outside D'Auria's bank on Seventh Avenue. Eventually Salvatore D'Auria was successful enough to have a street in the neighborhood named for himself.

Detail shot of Garside Street outside Michael Megaro's funeral home.
(Photo: Newark Public Library)

Tricolle Café at 43 Garside Street, circa 1915. It was called the Tricolle (three peaks) Cafe because its owner came from Ariano di Puglio. The proprietor, Francesco Paolo De Gennaro (with sleeves rolled up), sits in the doorway. Seated at right is his son, Joseph (Joe Barry) De Gennaro. (Photo: David Linfante)

Nicola Del Guercio poses outside his grocery store at 37 Garside Street, circa 1917. He was known as the "Watermelon King" of Garside Street. He also sold clams, which are displayed in the baskets at his feet. His wife, Maria Nicola Del Guercio, is visible behind the screen door. (Photo: Yola Schmidl)

TWO VIEWS OF A STOREFRONT AT 29 GARSIDE STREET:

Vincenzo D'Innocenzio in front of his coffee store at 29 Garside Street, circa 1922.
(Photo: Lucy D'Innocenzio)

Melillo's Fruit and Vegetable Market at the same address (29 Garside Street) several years later. (Photo: Gerald Melillo)

Benvenuta D'Innocenzio, circa 1926, in the doorway at 33 Garside Street after her husband's coffee store had relocated to that address.
(Photo: Lucy D'Innocenzio)

Francesco Esposito and son George pose in front of their barbershop at 18 Garside Street in 1926.
(Photo: Esposito Family)

On Garside Street and Factory Street lived a small group of families from the Italian-Albanian villages of San Giorgio Albanese and San Cosmo Albanese in Calabria. They spoke Albanian (Gheg) as well as Italian and were called Ghegi by their neighbors. Among them were the barber Francesco Esposito, the saloon keeper Filippo Zanfini, City Commissioner Anthony Minisi, the impresario Alfredo Cerrigone, who established the Newark Opera House, and the banker Scanderbeg Vangieri. Vangieri was a typical Italian banker who acted as a factotum for his neighbors, most of whom were poor and illiterate. He received their mail, sold steamship tickets, and served as a notary, thus gaining their trust. Then one day Vangieri absconded with their money.

Modesto Giordano (right) poses outside his bakery at 13 Garside Street in 1936 with his young assistants. Shown at his left are Joe Onofrietto, Fred Grasso, and Sam Giordano. Joe Onofrietto (Joe the Baker) worked as a counterboy at age ten and became a full-time baker at age sixteen. During the Depression his salary was eighteen dollars a week. He eventually owned the shop.
(Photo: Joe Onofrietto)

Francesco Esposito and wife Mariantonia in their backyard garden at 18 Garside Street in 1925. (Photo: Immerso Family)

Gerard Zanfini ("Jerry Gale") poses in his First Communion attire in 1921, outside his house at 17 Garside Street. His stories, recounting his early childhood growing up on Garside Street, were the inspiration for this book.
(Photo: Mary Zanfini)

Paolo Emilio De Rogatis poses outside the Teorese Club with other members. (Photo: Rose De Rogatis)

D'Auria's Bank at the corner of Garside Street and Seventh Avenue after the bank failed in 1936. D'Auria's Bank occupied a building that had once been the dormitory of the Old Soldier's Home. At one time, it housed the first Italian Baptist Mission in the United States. D'Auria's Bank was the First Ward's most important financial institution. Panic spread when the bank closed its doors during the "Bank Holiday" of 1933. D'Auria's bank was one of the first to reopen, but failed three years later. Eventually it was discovered that Mussolini was one of the bank's largest creditors. (Photo: UPI Bettmann Archive)

Shoeshine on Garside Street, circa 1930. Pictured are Joe Maglione, Ollie Caprio, and a man known as "Shine." (Photo: Connie De Gennaro)

Frank and Freddie Matullo pose beside the printing press at their father's print shop at 4 Garside Street. Pasquale Matullo printed several Italian-language newspapers including La Frusta, L'Ora, *and* Il Risviglio. *His son, Freddie, established the first office of the* Italian Tribune *at that address. It is still being published in Newark today.* (Photo: Tom Frien)

Mike Zarro poses in 1929 with his ice truck near his home at 75 Garside Street. The neighborhood depended on the horse and wagon for conveyance of most goods and services. Every morning the milk wagon came by. The milkman left his horse and wagon at the curb, and while he delivered the bottles, his horse walked slowly to the next stop and waited there. In the winter the milk froze in the milk boxes and cats licked the cream. When the ice wagon came to Garside Street everyone placed a sign in the window marked "10 cents" or "25 cents" to signal the iceman. He would hoist the ice up the steep tenement stairs with his ice tongs. The coal wagon, the ash wagon, and the beer wagon made regular stops on Garside Street. The coal yard was located on Orange Street near the Lackawanna train station and boys often took their sleds to the depot to get coal. The ash wagon came to collect the ash from the coal stoves. The ash was put out in big tin pails which lined the sidewalk outside the McKinley School on Factory Street, and during the winter months it was used to melt the snow and ice. (Photo: Diane Dunn)

Mother and children pose on the steps in the rear of a tenement. (Photo: Saint Lucy's Archives)

SIGHTS AND SOUNDS

The generation that grew up in the First Ward in those bygone days holds memories of sights, sounds, and smells that have not faded with the passage of time—the sound of horses' hooves on the ice-clogged cobblestones on Seventh Avenue, the call of the peddlers—"U Trippaiole!" and "U Pizzaiole!"—the smell of chocolate from the Brewster Chocolate Factory on Sheffield Street, and of wine during the wine-making season when grape crates were piled up high along the curbside. Entire families slept out on the fire escapes on sweltering summer nights and went with their neighbors to the Municipal Bathhouse on Clifton Avenue. There was no television, very little radio, just the pleasure of everyday life; and life in the neighborhood was public to an extraordinary degree.

Voices of peddlers filled the streets when they visited with their pushcarts and wagons. Zazzarino, a peddler of fancy meats (tripe, lungs, hearts, and livers), was known as "U Trippaiole." There was a ragman, "U Stracciare," who called out, "Any rags, any bones, any bottles, today?" and "U Pizzaiole," who peddled pizza on foot, decked out in a white baker's apron and a chef's hat. On his shoulder he balanced a copper tray, stacked with dozens of small pizzas and covered with a lid to keep them warm. He was a jovial fellow with a round face, white hair, and a white beard, and by the end of the day he was covered with sweat from head to foot. There was a garlic peddler from Boyden Street who carried his garlic in a sack slung over his shoulder, a Jewish pushcart peddler known as "Jack the Beanstalk" who sold pots and pans, and a "knife-and-scissors" man who came on foot with his grinding stone. Often a peddler would stop his wagon outside a building and call to his customer by name. Some customers wouldn't bother to come down if they lived up several steep flights of stairs. They would tie a rope to a basket and lower it to the street with a few coins in it. The peddler placed his produce in the basket and tugged on the rope.

Practically every building had a family-owned grocery store, a fruit and vegetable market, or a penny candy confectionery. Spezzaferro's Market on Seventh Avenue was famous for its parrot which warned the owner if a customer was trying to steal something. Spezzaferro (he was called "break iron" because of his great strength) kept his money in paper bags in the walls and floorboards of his market. After he died, his wife Rosina tore out the walls and found that most of it had been eaten by rats. But the parrot continued to guard the market and if a would-be thief appeared, it cried out in Italian, "Rosie, come quickly, they're stealing your fruit."

Many elements of Italian village life were present in the daily life of the neighborhood. Belief in *malocchio* (the evil eye) was common. A malady, such as a severe headache, was attributed to the influence of malocchio. A wise neighbor who knew how to break the spell was called upon in such circumstances. She would put a drop of hot oil into a dish, place her hand on the forehead of the sufferer and trace the sign of the cross to draw out the pain. As the children gathered around to watch, eyes wide in amazement, she began to moan and yawn. Her face would contort as sweat rolled down her neck. When the little bubble of oil in the dish burst, she had "broken" the malocchio.

The use of nicknames by almost everyone in the neighborhood was another custom carried over from the southern Italian villages where young men often bore the name of their grandfathers. Some towns had so many men with the same name that nicknames were a matter of necessity. One's profession, the size of one's nose, a physical deformity, the color of one's hair, a quirk, or a trait of one's personality provided one's nickname. Thus, the tripe peddler Zazzarino was "U Trippaiole," the one-legged grocer was Michele "U Zuppo" (cripple), the unkempt old woman became "U Zangara" (the witch), the dawdling peddler was "U Tardone," and the man who supplied the fireworks was "Soffiare su Fuoco" (fans the flame). Gangsters often acquired colorful monikers ("Sweat," "the Blade," "Billy Jinx"), and some neighbors only learned the true names of life-long acquaintances when they read them in the obituaries.

Every summer and fall, the First Ward had its grape season and its tomato season. During tomato season, when everyone prepared tomatoes for the year, empty tomato crates lined the streets and the heady smell of the sauce hung over the neighborhood. During grape season, the entire neighborhood smelled of fermenting wine. Families bought grapes at the freight yard on Orange Street and crushed them in a grinder (*maganillo*). They left them to ferment in the barrel for about a week and then drained the wine from the barrel and the residue went into the wine press (*u stringiadura*).

Few families owned a refrigerator, and women went to the Ice House on the corner of Sixth Avenue and Stone Street to collect blocks of ice for their ice boxes. They carried the blocks on their heads, balancing them on a towel to keep their heads from getting wet. Women used "leaf lard" rather than oil for cooking. They bought lard from the butcher or the pork store. They heated the lard in a frying pan, squeezing it dry until nothing remained except a few brittle bits, which were used for making ciccoli bread. Women made their own pasta (gli macaroni fatta mane). They used an iron needle to curl them and made noodles on a board with metal strings like a zither called a gittara. Few had ovens large enough for their baking needs. They prepared the dough at home and took it to the baker to bake in his oven and carried it home on a bread board they balanced on their head. Italian women washed their clothing with bleach called *biancolino* (white linens) that was sold by neighborhood peddlers. During the winter months, they hung their husbands' long johns out to dry on clotheslines, fastened between the tenement buildings where they froze, arms akimbo. The children marveled as the long johns slowly thawed and seemed to be lowering their arms.

The density of life in the neighborhood produced an extreme degree of social intimacy. Tenements often housed twenty or even thirty members of a single extended family, and neighbors residing in adjoining buildings had grown up side by side in the same village in Italy. This lent a provincial quality to the neighborhood where almost everyone was poor, where very few secrets were kept, and where every front stoop served as a village piazza. Neighbors knew they could count on each other in times of need. When the Great Depression struck, First Warders came to rely on each other even more than before. Life had always been hard; now every dime counted. Families and neighbors pulled together. Some used empty sacks of flour to make dresses, pillowcases, and bedsheets. One woman recounted that she and her twin brother were born in a macaroni box—"It was our crib." Many families had to go on some form of relief. Some obtained coal and firewood from a municipal distribution center on Clifton Avenue. Many turned to Reverend Perotti, pastor of Saint Lucy's Church, for assistance. He went from one shopkeeper to another to collect bread and meat for the poor who visited the rectory. Some brought their gas and electric bills to the pastor, which he promptly paid. Gang leader Richie Boiardo sent coal and baskets of food to poor families, often without their knowledge. Many shopkeepers kept a "butcher book" and people paid what they could. Eventually there were WPA jobs. Men found work draining the Morris Canal and paving streets. Families slowly got back on their feet, and through it all there was a deep sense of pride that "no one in the Ward went hungry."

Babe Tubello (on pony), with her brother Jimmy Tubello and his assistant Sam, in their backyard at 112 Eighth Avenue, circa 1920. The Tubello family operated a coal and ice company. During the Depression a load of coal cost three dollars for a quarter of a ton. "Some families could only afford twenty-five cents," she recalls, "But my mother made sure that everyone got their next delivery." (Photo: Mildred Avitable)

Rafaello Nicastro and his son Toby pose with their truck in 1932 near the corner of Factory Street and Drift Street. McKinley School is in the background. (Photo: Dolores Nicastro)

Couple strolling through Branch Brook Park; the Cathedral of the Sacred Heart, under construction, is visible in the background. The park, designed by the Olmsted Brothers in 1901 and covering over 270 acres, was the first county park in America. The Morris Canal originally formed its western boundary. The cathedral, fifth largest in the United States, covers an area of 40,000 square feet, comparable in size to Westminster Abbey in London. Its towers rise to a height of 232 feet (28 feet higher than Notre Dame of Paris). Groundbreaking for the cathedral took place in January 1898, and a crowd of more than 100,000 witnessed the laying of its cornerstone in June 1899. It was completed in 1954. Pope John Paul II visited the cathedral in 1995 and elevated it to the rank of basilica minor. *The couple shown above are Andrew and Carmella Napolitano.* (Photo: Saint Lucy's Archives)

Baptismal party at the home of Rodolfo and Assunta Colamedici on Cutler Street in 1925 for their daughter Theresa Colamedici. Rodolfo Colamedici was a photographer who owned Rudolph's Photo Studio at 71 Seventh Avenue. (Photo: Theresa Colamedici)

Children growing up in the First Ward attended several neighborhood schools, including Franklin School, Webster Street School, Seventh Avenue Elementary School, and McKinley Middle School. Six thousand children (about eleven thousand under thirteen resided in the neighborhood) were enrolled in the mid-1920s. The overwhelming majority were Italian. After school, those who did not have a part-time job to earn a few pennies played together in the playgrounds, on the stoops, in alleys, and in the streets. Boys played caddy and shot "aggies." Girls played "landy," a form of hopscotch. Curbside bonfires served up husks of corn, or potatoes cooked in their skins until they were hard and black. There were candy apples from the Jelly Apple Man, Italian ices from Castellano's horse-drawn lemon ice wagon, and hot sweet potatoes from U Fumo, the sweet potato peddler. Often street performers visited the neighborhood. The famous street singer Arthur Tracy, later a radio and recording artist, frequently performed on the corner of Sixth Avenue. There was a legless, singing beggar who wheeled himself along Seventh Avenue on a wooden platform singing through a megaphone, and an organ grinder with his monkey—the monkey would tip his hat if you gave him a coin. Children awaited the arrival of "u dula-dula" (a horse drawn merry-go-round), or gathered outside Dietsch's Restaurant, a popular dinner and dance club near the corner of Clifton Avenue and Bloomfield Avenue frequented by Hollywood movie stars like Marlene Dietrich, Barbara Stanwyck, and Cesar Romero, and where the doorman wore an Italian *bersaglieri* uniform.

Italian children got to celebrate American holidays such as the Fourth of July, as well as traditional feasts and saints' days, with bursts of fireworks; exploding rockets often lit up Drift Street. In the summertime, boys went swimming in the Morris Canal at "Bare-Ass Beaches" along the edge of Branch Brook Park. If something went awry, one of them would cry out, "Jinjo got you!" It was a way of saying that no misdeed goes unpunished.

McKinley Elementary School class photo, circa 1924. (Photo: Daniel Fabrizio)

Children at play in the First Ward during the 1920s (opposite page) as depicted in rotogravure photographs which appeared in the Sunday Call. *Two decades later, in the 1940s, the First Ward got its first Boys Club. The Eighth Avenue Boys Club, the first of its kind in the city, occupied a converted factory at the corner of High Street.*

Children photographed on rear steps of a tenement on Eighth Avenue in 1924. (Photo: *Sunday Call* 11/2/1924)

Unidentified group of children, photographed in 1924. (Photo: *Sunday Call* 11/9/1924)

Children playing in an improvised swimming pool outside the firehouse on Mount Prospect Avenue in 1921. (Photo: *Sunday Call* 8/14/1921)

The Municipal Bathhouse on Clifton Avenue in Branch Brook Park, near the corner of Seventh Avenue. The bathhouse had forty-eight showers for men, twenty-seven for women, and sixteen small tubs for children under ten. Many flats lacked indoor plumbing and thousands showered for free (a towel was provided for a penny) at the bathhouse. Everyone was allotted three minutes in the shower. An attendant with a stick came by and banged on the door. "Time's up!" he would shout. (Photo: Newark Public Library)

Children pose outside the Clifton Avenue Bathhouse in 1925. (Photo: Newark Public Library)

Tubs used for bathing babies at the Clifton Avenue Bathhouse, 1923. (Photo: Newark Public Library)

CLIFTON AVENUE BATHOUSE

A common sight at the bathhouse is to see an entire family, ranging from grandfather to grandchildren, arriving for their baths; for the bathhouse is made use of equally by all generations of Italians. Many Italian mothers come daily with their children to bathe, their desire exceeding their actual need, according to the attendant.

However, the bathhouse is used by all nationalities and races in complete unity and respect for each other. Each person will wait his or her turn to enter a shower, and there are times when persons have had to wait as long as an hour or even more, but this has not caused any trouble to any of the attendants as yet. The many different nationalities always seem to be in a good mood and get along well with each other. While disorders of any kind are immediately curtailed and offenders are liable to arrest, most people who use the bathhouse have a sense of appreciation for its existence.

According to the attendant interviewed, there are about six thousand persons who use the bathhouse weekly. Of this number, the Italians outnumber all others by about two to one. This is because of its location on Clifton Avenue, in the center of the First Ward, which is predominantly Italian.

—Description of Clifton Avenue bathhouse from an ethnic survey conducted by the Federal Writers' Project

Family-owned businesses were the lifeblood of the neighborhood. They occupied almost every available space, no matter how cramped, including tenement basements and rear tenement buildings (which often housed chicken markets), and it is hard to imagine the First Ward without them.

Many shopkeepers started out as laborers who scraped together enough money to rent a little space and, unless they had a particular trade, would try their hand at almost anything. If they could not make a go of one thing, they would try something else. Some shops changed hands so quickly, they are hardly remembered. But many survived and some shopkeepers became quite prosperous. Some lasted as long as they did because of the way shopping was conducted in the neighborhood. No one had much money and everyone benefited by having it constantly circulate. A mother sent her daughter to buy some greens from the grocer in their building, a soup bone from the butcher down the street, a few apples from a market on Seventh Avenue, and some potatoes from a peddler who happened by. Often no actual money changed hands. The transaction was noted in a butcher book, the account to be settled at a later date. This not only kept the shopkeeper in business and his family from starving, it also created an important underpinning within the neighborhood. When the Great Depression came, shopkeepers were able to return the favor. If a shopkeeper knew his customer had no money, he would put something extra into the bag and refuse to take "no" for an answer.

Shopkeepers who built a good reputation could do a fantastic business. Their clientele was not limited to their neighbors. It included a vast number of people whose families had moved to less crowded Italian neighborhoods, and also those who were drawn to the First Ward's Little Italy because of its bakeries, fish markets, pastry shops, butchershops, and fruit and vegetable markets.

Alfred and Jerry Frungillo in their market at 97 Mount Prospect Avenue in 1929. (Photo: Frungillo Family)

Filomena Celentano poses with her children Ann, Louise, Tommy, and Armando, outside Celentano's Market at 99 Seventh Avenue, circa 1925. Her husband, Antonio Celentano, came from Sorrento where his family was in the dairy product (latticini) *business. He arrived in Newark at the turn of the century and opened a* latteria *on Seventh Avenue, producing his own products—mozzarella, ricotta, scarmorza—in the backroom of his store. His daughter Anna had a small macaroni factory on Wood Street. Since her father disliked square ravioli, Anna made round ravioli, cutting them by hand with an empty can of tomato paste. When his brother John came to Newark, Antonio helped him establish his own business on Fourteenth Avenue. John proposed they become partners in the macaroni business and acquire machinery from Italy to mass produce the ravioli. Antonio declined, but John went ahead anyway. Eventually John's sons opened Celentano Brothers' Market on Eighth Avenue. Today the company is headquartered in Verona, New Jersey. The round ravioli became Celentano's trademark; they have sold in the millions.* (Photo: Celentano Family)

Nunzio Sica (in white shirt) and wife Virginia pose with customers outside their vegetable market at 146 High Street, circa 1930. (Photo: Sica Family)

Tony Fragasso poses outside McKinley Market at 196 Eighth Avenue, circa 1920. His sisters Jennie and Nettie are visible in the doorway. (Photo: Jeanette Fragasso Masi)

Joseph and Josephine Mascellino pose in front of their bakery shop at 220 Eighth Avenue in 1926. (Photo: Palmina Mascellino)

The Parisi family, circa 1930, photographed inside their shoe store at 111 Seventh Avenue. (Photo: *Italian Tribune*)

Michael Siciliano and his daughter Fanny in their candy store at 11 Sheffield Street, circa 1925. (Photo: Fanny De Donna)

The Suppa brothers, circa 1928, outside their decorations factory at 36 Sheffield Street, at work preparing decorations for the feast of Saint Michael. (Photo: Lena Papa)

Teddy Corbo outside his monument shop at 10 Boyden Street, circa 1925. (Photo: Jean Della Ventura)

De Carlo's Garage at 88 Nesbitt Street. (Photo: Dr. Frank Alfano)

Vincenzo Fragasso with members of his circle in the bocce alley at the rear of Fragasso's restaurant at 194 Eighth Avenue, circa 1928. (Photo: Jeanette Fragasso Masi)

Group of boys on the steps of the Miniature Incandescent Lamp Factory, at the corner of High Street and Eighth Avenue, in 1920. It later became the Tung-Sol Factory. At one time it employed six hundred people, half of them from the First Ward.
(Photo: Thomas Pallante)

Bakers pose inside Arre's Italian Tasty Crust Bakery at 128 Eighth Avenue in 1938.
(Photo: Theresa Racanelli)

Columbia Ruglio, photographed in her backyard on Seventh Avenue, holding her granddaughter Dolores, who is dressed for Halloween, circa 1922.
(Photo: Camille N. Ruglio)

Lower Eighth Avenue near Summer Avenue, facing west, photographed in 1935.
(Photo: Mildred Avitable)

Beatrice family poses in their restaurant at 92 Seventh Avenue, circa 1928. Sabina is at the right, Arthur to the left, and Edna is the second from the left. (Photo: Stephen Yasko)

Monsignor Joseph Perotti (center), circa 1920, with Reverend Gaetano Ruggiero (right), and Reverend Serafino Donzillo. (Photo: Saint Lucy's Archives)

THE CHURCH

Saint Lucy's Church on Sheffield Street was the First Ward's spiritual axis and remains its most enduring institution. The parish was established in 1891. Originally a small, wood-frame structure, a mission rather than a full-fledged parish church, Saint Lucy's grew to become a national parish with forty thousand Italians in its jurisdiction. In 1925 the old church was torn down and replaced with a magnificent new Saint Lucy's Church.

The role Saint Lucy's parish played in the early history of the First Ward reflects the centrality of the Catholic Church in southern Italy where village-based solidarity (*campanilismo*) was measured by proximity to the bell tower (*campanile*) of the local church. Southern Italians expressed their faith through devotion to the patron saint of their town (*paese*), especially on the saint's feast day when the statue was carried in procession from the church through the village. These processions were faithfully recreated by the southern Italian townsfolk who settled in the First Ward. By serving as a repository for the statues brought over from Italy and by gathering parishioners from many different Italian towns into a single parish, the church was gradually transforming the southern Italian immigrant. Those who heretofore had regarded themselves as Calabrittani or Teorese began to think of themselves as Italian Americans. At the same time, the parish church was becoming the hub of a social unit that was completely foreign to the

southern Italian *contadini* (rural laborer) who had never before visited a large city—the urban neighborhood.

The evolution of Saint Lucy's parish during its first half-century is largely the story of two priests, two very different men: the saintly Monsignor Joseph Perotti and his strong-willed successor, the Reverend Gaetano Ruggiero. Perotti was born in northern Italy in 1867. He came to the United States in 1894 and served briefly at parishes in New York and Boston before coming to Saint Lucy's where he was appointed pastor in 1897. The little parish was deeply in debt then, but Perotti was committed to lifting his countrymen out of the squalor and poverty in which he found them. His greatest concern was for the countless Italian children in his parish and, despite the mounting debt, he was determined to establish a parish school. Perotti sought assistance from Mother Frances Xavier Cabrini. Mother Cabrini, the first American citizen canonized by the Church, had already organized a school at Our Lady of Mount Carmel parish in Newark's Ironbound quarter, where she was known as "Santina." The Missionary Sisters of the Sacred Heart, under Mother Cabrini's direction, came to Saint Lucy's in 1902 to establish the new school. However, even this future saint could not overcome the poverty of the parish, and after one year the school was abandoned. That same year a fire damaged the church. Perotti made several more attempts to secure a school. He finally succeeded in 1906 when the Sisters of Saint John established a residence for their order at Saint Lucy's Church and took charge of the project.

Perotti then turned his attention to the task of building a new church. The parish had long outgrown the little wood-frame structure, and Perotti began to implore and cajole the bishop for a new church. By 1920 the parish census stood at seventeen thousand. More than 10,000 baptisms had been performed during the previous decade; 1,110 were recorded in a single year. Perotti's flock was becoming impatient, but the pastor faced a difficult problem. The feasts celebrated by the people with such fervor were organized by societies that were outside the control of the church. The people, although quite poor, supported them generously, but the church reaped little financial benefit from the feasts. The church was starving. Perotti wanted to suspend the feasts while raising money for the new church but was prevented from doing so. Although he had no money, he went ahead with his plans and in 1923, he built a parish hall to serve as a temporary place of worship while the new church was being constructed. Two years later, the old church was demolished and groundbreaking commenced for the new church, which was consecrated on the Feast of Saint Lucy, December 13, 1926. The interior remained unfinished. At first it had no windows, and the birds flew in during mass.

The Great Depression forced Perotti to suspend plans for completion of the interior of the church. He now devoted all his energy and resources to the poor of

the parish, and no one who came to him went away empty-handed. In 1929 he established the Saint Vincent de Paul Society to assist the needy. Two years later, he was elevated to the rank of monsignor. In 1933 he completed a new building to house the Italian Catholic Union; however, that same year he collapsed while celebrating mass. He died on September 14, 1933. The entire First Ward mourned Perotti's death. Three thousand people crowded into Saint Lucy's Church for the funeral mass and thousands more lined the streets outside. "We are burying a saint today," Bishop Walsh declared in his eulogy, and he invited anyone who doubted this to visit the bare room where Perotti had resided. Those who had worked at his side described Perotti as a man who "carried his charity to its ultimate end," and who literally gave everything he had to the poor. Indeed, when he was elevated to the office of monsignor, he had no money to pay for his new vestments. At the time of his death, his only possessions were fifty cents and the clothes on his back. Perotti was buried at Holy Sepulcher Cemetery in a grave donated by two parishioners. During his tenure, Saint Lucy's had grown from two thousand to thirty-five thousand members.

Perotti did not live to complete the church. The task fell to his successor, the Reverend Gaetano Ruggiero, who was appointed pastor in 1934. He had been Perotti's assistant from 1922 to 1931 and had become his closest friend. But the two men were strikingly different. Ruggiero was Sicilian. He was a doctor of Canon Law and had served as a chaplain in the Italian army. He was more worldly than his predecessor and he was exceptionally strong-willed. Ruggiero moved quickly to assert his authority. One of his first acts was to insist that henceforth all feasts would be conducted under the control of the church. Despite vehement objections, including a threat against his life, Ruggiero prevailed. He was able to complete the interior of the church in just six months.

Saint Lucy's Church, as completed by the Reverend Ruggiero, is an iconic map in stone, plaster, and glass of the hilltop towns and villages of southern Italy from which the people of the First Ward came. The statues and windows that decorate the church bear the names of a dozen towns from Avellino, Potenza, Salerno, and Caserta provinces which were the wellspring of migration to the First Ward at the beginning of this century. Each statue had at one time been lovingly brought over from Italy and was the object of a special devotion on its feast day, when it was carried from the church in a colorful procession. On that day the church echoed with the voices of women singing the rhythmic and repetitive *cantileni* and was resplendent with the glow of hundreds of tiny candles. Today almost no one can recall the distant time when Saint Sabino and Saint Sebastiano had their feasts, but their statues remain, a record and a reminder of the immigrant roots of this vanished neighborhood.

Ruggiero guided and sustained Saint Lucy's parish through the remainder of

The original wood-frame Saint Lucy's Church on Sheffield Street, erected in 1892. Saint Lucy's parish was established in 1891 by the Reverend Conrad Schotthoeffer, a German priest fluent in Italian, who was dispatched to Newark to organize parishes in the city's Italian districts. Reverend Felix Morelli, who participated in the formation of Italian parishes in Newark and New York City, served as Saint Lucy's first administrator. The parish celebrated its one hundredth anniversary in 1991. (Photo: Saint Lucy's Archives)

the depression years and throughout the Second World War. His tenure spanned the First Ward's heyday as well as some of its saddest moments. While some considered him an old-style Italian pastor, who could be at times strict and domineering, he is remembered by most as a kind and caring priest and a skillful administrator. He was the preeminent figure in the community for more than three decades. His insistence that the feasts be held under the auspices of the church, assured the survival of the parish, by securing a source of income when the number of active parishioners began to decline. But, ironically, his decision to support urban renewal, as shall be seen, hastened the neighborhood's demise. He served as Saint Lucy's pastor for thirty-two years, until his death in 1966. He was succeeded by Monsignor Joseph Granato, the present pastor, who served as his assistant for twelve years. There is thus an unbroken chain from Perotti to Granato which spans an entire century.

Boys pose in the yard at old Saint Lucy's Church, circa 1915.
(Photo: Ralph Pellecchia)

Saint Lucy's School, faculty and students, circa 1925. The school is still in operation.
(Photo: Loretta Castellano)

Saint Joseph's Council of the Italian Catholic Union (ICU) outside the ICU headquarters at the corner of Seventh Avenue and Amity Place in 1928. The Reverend Perotti established the ICU in 1919. It became the largest organization in the First Ward with over 1,200 members.
(Photo: Margaret Linarducci)

Despite the extreme poverty of the parish during the early decades of his tenure, Perotti was able to nurture and sustain his flock. He often disbursed his entire salary as pastor to meet monthly obligations because the parish wasconstantly in debt. But he was unwavering in his determination to build a parish school. "I wanted with all my heart," he wrote in 1904, "to do something for the new coming Italian generations." He not only succeeded in establishing the school, he also built a new parish hall, organized youth programs, established the Italian Catholic Union, initiated programs to assist the poor, and eventually built the new church. It was said that "he really could work miracles." And yet, Perotti did not even own the rectory he lived in on Eighth Avenue and he was incapable of spending money for his own care. When the bishop heard that Perotti needed dental work, he ordered his assistant to accompany the pastor to the dentist, but not to give him the money, because Perotti would simply give it away.

The Reverend Perotti poses with Saint Lucy's Fife, Drum, and Bugle Corps, circa 1925.
(Photo: Judy Mascenzo)

CHILDREN (BELOW) FROM SAINT LUCY'S PARISH DRESSED FOR FIRST COMMUNION AND CONFIRMATION. GIRLS WORE WHITE GOWNS WITH DISTINCTIVE FLORAL HEADDRESSES.

Anthony Nittoli, Mamie Nittoli, and Fred Nittoli pose in their Confirmation outfits, circa 1910. (Photo: James Lecky)

Julia Clemente, circa 1915, in First Communion gown.
(Photo: Anna Lombardi)

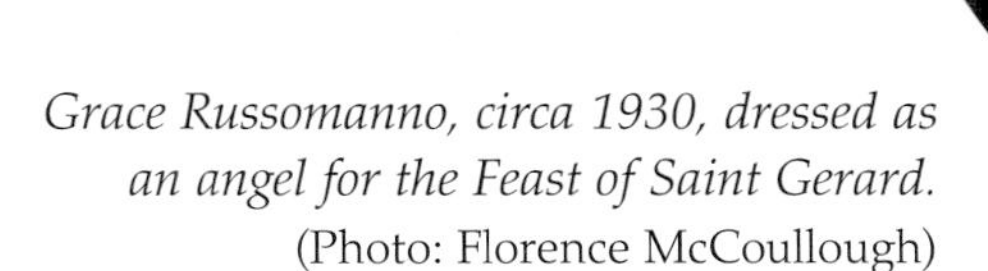

Grace Russomanno, circa 1930, dressed as an angel for the Feast of Saint Gerard.
(Photo: Florence McCoullough)

Groundbreaking ceremony for Saint Lucy's Church, May 3, 1925. (Photo: Saint Lucy's Archives)

Nicolo Zarro poses in the uniform of the Italian Catholic Union. (Photo: Angela Raimo)

Bishop Thomas Walsh at the official dedication ceremony of the new Saint Lucy's Church, July 22, 1928. (Photo: Saint Lucy's Archives)

Plan of St. Lucy's Church

Saints venerated at Saint Lucy's Church and towns in Italy (shown in parentheses) which brought the devotion to the First Ward.

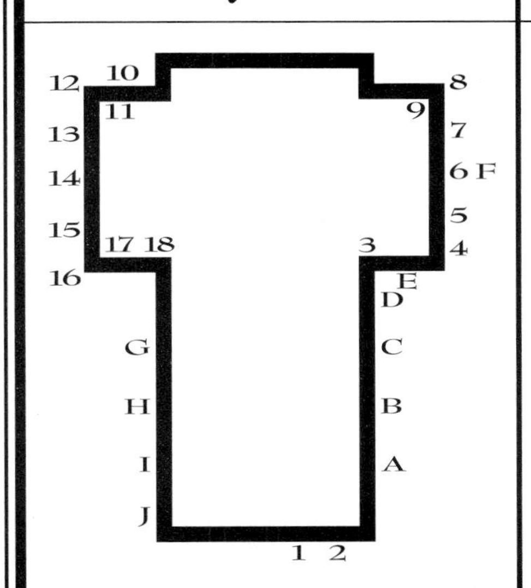

STATUES

1 Saint Lucy
2 Maria Addolorata
3 Saint Vito (Castelgrande)
4 Maria Incoronata [I] (Recigliano)
5 Maria dell' Assunta di Pierno (San Fele)
6 Our Lady of Mount Carmel (Avigliano)
7 Saint Sabino (Atripalda)
8 Saint Anne
9 Saint Nicolo (Tèora)
10 Saint Gerard Maiella Chapel (Caposele)
11 Saint Rocco (Lioni)
12 Saint Sebastiano (Marigliano)
13 Maria della Neve (Calabritto)
14 Saint Joseph
15 Maria Incoronata [II] (Sant' Andrea di Conza)
16 Saint Donato
17 Saint Anthony
18 Saint Michael (Maddaloni)

WINDOWS

A Saint Michael
B Saint Nicolo
C Saint Mark (Manocalzati)
D Maria Addolorata
E Our Lady of Mount Carmel
F Saint Lucy
G Saint Sabino
H Maria della Neve
I Saint Anthony
J Saint Rocco

Saint Lucy's Church and adjacent buildings along Sheffield Street just prior to completion in 1926. Perotti died before completing the interior of the church. He left it with bare walls, removable chairs instead of pews, and a wooden altar. Ruggiero completed the interior in 1934. The present day decorations, including the marble columns, stained glass windows, and ceiling paintings, were completed in 1948 under the direction of Gonippo Raggi, whose work included the interior ornamentation for Sacred Heart Cathedral. (Photo: Saint Lucy's Archives)

Interior of Saint Lucy's Church during a nuptial mass, circa 1930. (Photo: Saint Lucy's Archives)

Perotti poses in front of the grand Neapolitan Christmas presepio at Saint Lucy's Church, circa 1928. The presepio depicts the birth of Christ with all the traditional elements of the Christmas story. The setting, however, is a Neapolitan village teeming with life. Saint Lucy's presepio, with more than one hundred terra-cotta and cloth figures, handmade in Italy, was the creation of Luigi Penza, the church sexton for more than fifty years. The preparation of the presepio is a Christmas tradition still preserved at Saint Lucy's Church. Each year on Christmas Eve, at midnight mass, the church is filled to overflowing. (Photo: Theresa Colamedici)

Sisters of Saint John during a procession on Sheffield Street in 1948 to mark the reopening of the church following completion of interior decorations. The order established its first American residence at Saint Lucy's Church in 1906 and recently celebrated its ninetieth anniversary.
(Photo: Saint Lucy's Archives)

Women pose on steps outside Saint Lucy's Church.
(Photo: Maria Casale D'Alessio)

The Reverend Gaetano Ruggiero (right) with Bishop Walsh during the procession prior to the rededication of Saint Lucy's Church. Ruggiero inherited an enormous debt from Perotti, but he very quickly placed the parish on a firm financial footing. (Photo: Saint Lucy's Archives)

Feast of Saint Gerard in 1914, photographed at the corner of Garside Street and Sixth Avenue. The constable at right is Ottone Genuario. (Photo: Genuario Family)

FEASTS

Life in the overwhelmingly Roman Catholic First Ward was guided by faith, custom, and ritual. This was most dramatically reflected in the number of feasts celebrated in the neighborhood, some of which predated the founding of Saint Lucy's Church. The feasts brought the traditional devotion to the saints and the festive spirit of the Italian village to the urban immigrant neighborhood. From June to October, the First Ward celebrated a feast practically every other week. Each town that was represented in sufficient numbers organized one to honor its patron saint. The Teorese venerated Saint Nicolo, the Lionese honored Saint Rocco, the Atripaldese celebrated Saint Sabino, Our Lady of the Assumption (La Madonna Assunta di Pienro) was honored as patroness of San Fele, and Our Lady of Snows was venerated by the Calabrittani. The feast of Our Lady of Snows had been celebrated with a procession through the neighborhood as early as 1888.

The feasts attracted controversy when they first appeared in Newark's Italian enclaves. They were often described as pagan and irreligious, and the festivities were not without incidents. Saint Rocco's feast in 1891 was marred by a dreadful tragedy when a copper casing filled with fireworks exploded outside Alfonso Ilaria's saloon on Boyden Street. Seven people were killed and fifty were injured.

There were numerous attempts to outlaw the feasts, and a stabbing in 1906 prompted the chief of police to suspend them. Some Italians, decrying the "so-called religious festivals," wanted them banned altogether. But efforts to suppress the feasts did not succeed, and they continued to grow as increasing numbers of Italians settled in the First Ward.

Individual guilds and societies oversaw the various details and preparations for the feasts. Some tasks were handed down through several generations within the same family. The church had to be cleaned and decorated, and special care was devoted to the statue of the saint in preparation of the feast day. Saint Gerard was robed in a new set of clothes every year and strips from the previous year were distributed as relics, a practice that continues today. During Saint Rocco's procession, the statue wore a solid gold, wide-brimmed pilgrim's hat, made from donated wedding rings and jewelry. The cost of conducting the feast was borne by the society, which hired a band, created the decorations, arranged for the panegirico (a special homily honoring the saint), and provided fireworks.

The narrow streets surrounding Saint Lucy's Church were adorned with arches of multicolored electric lights (*lampadine*) and small baskets of flowers. At one time the colorful street arches were lighted with glass globes containing oil wicks. Sometimes the church facade was decorated with an elaborate replica of the hometown church, fashioned out of paper, tinsel, and wood. A grandstand festooned with red, white, and green bunting was erected on Sheffield Street outside the church, where bands played and dignitaries addressed the crowd. Small concession stands called bancarelli lined the streets offering Italian delicacies such as *mogiadelle* (innards cooked on a spit), *torrone* (glazed candy), clams, mussels, sausages, nuts, and other treats. The torrone was fashioned into a big block and was so hard it had to be cut with an ax. There were game stands, amusements, and carnival rides along D'Auria Street. At night, concert bands and orchestras played, and singers performed opera and Neapolitan songs. There were nightly fireworks displays including a pyrotechnic effect that reproduced the saint's face and always stirred the crowd.

The procession with the statue of the saint was the emotional high point of the feast. A guard of honor led the procession, followed by the priests, altar boys, and the band. Thousands took part in the processions. Some carried large candles. Some walked barefoot or in stockinged feet. Others carried children in their arms. The procession moved slowly, stopping along the way at improvised shrines or where a photograph of the saint was displayed in a window or on a fire escape. Sometimes baskets of flowers were lowered from the fire escapes and capes covered with dollar bills were draped around the statue. People also gave gold wedding bands, watch chains, rings, earrings, and other jewelry which were hung on the statue and then placed in the "gold box" that was also carried in the procession. At every stop, the saint's devotees stood before the statue, recited a prayer or engaged in a public conversation with the saint. Doves were sometimes released, and the statue was showered with flower petals. Then the band played and the procession moved on to the next stop. In the course of several days, every corner of the neighborhood was visited. At the end of each procession, the money was removed from the statue before it reentered the church and was kept by the society that had sponsored the feast. Only donations received inside the church were considered church property. This practice was in force until the Reverend Ruggiero took charge of the feasts around 1935.

The annual season of feasts at Saint Lucy's Church began with Saint Anthony's Feast on June 13, when the poles for the lights illuminating the streets went up, and culminated in the Feast of Saint Gerard on October 16. Saint Anthony was revered by all and his feast was universally celebrated. Saint Gerard, patron of Caposele, was venerated as protector of mothers and his feast was the grandest of all. It is still celebrated at Saint Lucy's Church. Most impressive, perhaps, was the feast in honor of Saint Michael the Archangel, patron of Maddaloni. Twice during this procession, girls dressed as angels were suspended from ropes attached to the fire escapes and glided above the heads of the crowd as the statue passed by. Feasts were also held in Newark's other large Italian enclaves, at Saint Rocco's Church on Fourteenth Avenue and Our Lady of Mount Carmel Church in the Ironbound district.

Special processions marked holy days such as the Feast of Corpus Christi on the first Sunday in June. For the Corpus Christi procession, the fire escapes and windows along Seventh Avenue and Eighth Avenue were decorated with bed sheets, blankets, and bedspreads which were blessed by the priests. Each family displayed its most beautiful linens, and special altars were erected along the procession route.

The great feasts of Easter and Christmas were observed with traditional customs. During Holy Week, the statues at Saint Lucy's Church were covered as a sign of mourning until midday on Holy Saturday when the ringing of the church bells signaled the end of the Easter fast. The centerpiece of the traditional Easter meal was *cappretto* (baby lamb). At Christmas time, an enormous Neapolitan presepio was erected at Saint Lucy's Church, and every vendor on Seventh Avenue, Cutler Street, and Sheffield Street sold eel for *La Vigilia* (the Christmas vigil) when Italians abstained from eating meat. Eel was the mainstay of the traditional Christmas Eve dinner when custom demanded that thirteen different food items grace the table. After the meal, the family gathered at Saint Lucy's Church for midnight mass and the Christmas Eve procession. Italian bagpipe players led the candlelight procession with the figure of the *Bambino*. A band accompanied the procession and people sang the Italian Christmas carol called the *Pastorale*. The procession visited almost every street in the neighborhood before returning to the church to place the figure of the infant in the *presepio*.

Feast of Saint Sabino, patron of Atripalda, on Sheffield Street, circa 1890. Participants carry a tower (described variously as a gilio *or* staniare*) composed of several tiers of small candles forming a single large candle.* (Photo: Frances San Giovanni)

Members of Saint Gerard Committee pose on Eighth Avenue near corner of Nesbitt Street, circa 1915. (Photo: Camille N. Ruglio)

Feast of Saint Anthony, 1906. Photograph was reproduced from a glass negative.
(Photo: Saint Lucy's Archives)

Members of the Societa San Marco Evangelista pose, circa 1910, in front of an elaborately decorated stage, erected at the corner of Eighth Avenue and Factory Street, honoring the patron of the village of Monocalzati. The display is a replica of the facade of the actual church. (Photo: George Malanga)

Procession on Garside Street during the Feast of San Nicolo in 1918. Flower girls (Mary Cella, left, and Mary Milano Del Guercio, right) carry a tower composed of hundreds of small candles decorated with a picture of San Nicolo, patron of Teora. Saint Lucy's parish was terribly poor, so the candles were donated to the church at the end of the feast and were almost a year's supply. (Photo: Rose De Rogatis; Rose Di Vincenzo)

Feast of Saint Gerard

The most important and most enduring feast held in the First Ward was the Feast of San Gerardo Maiella, patron of Caposele, celebrated every sixteenth of October. The bond between Saint Gerard and the Italians of the First Ward reflects a common history shared by the saint and the people who venerate him. Gerardo Maiella was born in Muro Lucano in 1726. He lived and worked among the Avellinese and remains part of the collective memory of the community. He died in 1755 and his body is entombed at the monastery of Materdomini, on the outskirts of Caposele. When the first processions honoring him took place in Newark, he was not yet a saint (he was canonized in 1904) and was addressed as "Beato Gerardo." The earliest manifestation of devotion to Saint Gerard in the First Ward is attributed to Alfonso Alfone and his wife Maria Giuseppe Alfone, who came to in Newark in 1887. Maria Alfone brought a picture of Gerardo Maiella from Italy and began the custom of carrying the picture through the streets of the neighborhood. Her husband was a founder of the Caposelese society which initiated the feast. In 1898 the Caposelese sent to Italy for a life-size statue of Gerardo Maiella. The day the ship arrived, they went to Hoboken to pick up the statue. At the dock, they approached the shipmaster and explained in Italian that they had come for Gerardo Maiella. He examined the register and found no one by that name. "Gerardo Maiella is not on this ship," he replied. After a few moments of confusion the matter was untangled and the statue of Gerardo Maiella was on its way to Newark.

Saint Gerard was venerated as the patron of mothers and it was customary to pray to him if a woman had difficulty in childbirth or was unable to conceive. If the prayers were answered, the child was sometimes named Gerard in honor of the saint and was carried in its mother's arms during the procession. Sometimes the child was dressed in a black robe in homage to the saint. Women also donned black robes during the procession. Devotees vowed to perform acts of penance in return for particular favors. Some walked in the procession in bare feet. Others came on their knees to the niche where the statue was displayed, and some even licked the ground as they approached the statue.

By 1920 the devotion to Saint Gerard had grown to such proportions that a new organization, the Societa Maschile San Gerardo Maiella (Saint Gerard Men's Society), was formed to conduct the annual feast. The Saint Gerard Chapel was completed in 1935, and in 1977 Saint Lucy's Church was officially designated "National Shrine of Saint Gerard." The Newark *Sunday Call* occasionally published rotogravure photographs of feasts held at Saint Lucy's Church during the 1920s and 1930s. Various elements of the Feast of Saint Gerard are depicted in the photographs on the following pages.

Feast of Saint Gerard in 1935. Close-up shot of statue draped in capes of money.
(Photo: *Sunday Call* 10/27/1935)

Girls dressed for the procession during the Feast of Saint Gerard in 1923.
(Photo: *Sunday Call* 10/28/1923)

Members of the Women's Auxiliary of the Saint Gerard's Guild, photographed in 1924.
(Photo: *Sunday Call* 11/2/1924)

During Saint Gerard's Feast in 1924 a basket decorated with flowers, dollar bills, and ribbons is lowered from a line attached to the fire escape as the procession halts in front of a building.
(Photo: *Sunday Call* 11/2/1924)

A woman carries a candle during the Feast of Saint Gerard in 1924. The size or weight of the candles carried in the procession would sometimes be equal to the weight or size of the person, often a child, for whom the saint was asked to intercede.
(Photo: *Sunday Call* 11/2/1924)

The two images reproduced below are individual frames from a 9.5 mm home movie of a Feast of Saint Gerard made during the 1920s.

Women's Auxiliary with banner during the procession. (Photo: Nicholas Melillo)

Women carry the "gold box" during the procession. In addition to contributing money, people often donated gold rings, wedding bands, watch chains, earrings and other jewelry which were hung on the statue and then later placed in the gold box. (Photo: Nicholas Melillo)

The little Italian Catholic Church of Saint Lucy was the center of festivities last Thursday. All along Sheffield Street, on either side, in front of the church, the festival booths were arranged and the crowd of Italian folks, in holiday garb, surged up and down the narrow thoroughfare, purchasing Italian nuts and sweetmeats, watching the magician make the devil dance up and down a glass tube, and listening to the strains of the hurdy-gurdy pounding out Italian music. . . . One of the principal features of the day is the procession, made up of various Catholic Italian societies, headed by the priests of the Church of Saint Lucy and other Italian Catholic churches in the city. One of the prettiest features of the procession is the company of virginella, little girls who give a rare touch to the scene, and remind one of old-world paintings of great religious occasions. The girls carry candles and wear white dresses with bared heads.

—*Sunday Call* 8/18/1901

Procession during Feast of Saint Gerard in 1927. The Reverend Gaetano Ruggiero is at left. (Photo: *Sunday Call* 10/23/1927)

"Flight of Angels" during the procession of the Feast of Saint Michael in 1939. The highlight of the procession in honor of the patron of Maddaloni was a traditional salute to the archangel called volo de gli angeli—the flight of the angels. It took place at the beginning and end of the procession. The "angels" were little girls dressed in white gowns, fitted with a small harness concealed under their wings, who were suspended by ropes attached to the fire escapes. Each carried a basket. As the procession approached, men on the fire escapes hoisted the angels onto the ropes which stretched from one side of the street to the other. The ropes were drawn by means of a pulley so that the angels appeared to be flying over the heads of the crowd below. The angels quieted the crowd by calling out: "Silenzio! Silenzio!" The procession came to a halt and the angels recited a prayer ending with the words: "Viva San Michele!" "Viva San Michele!" the crowd roared back. The angels then saluted Saint Michael with flower petals and released doves concealed in their baskets. The crowd applauded and fireworks exploded in the street. The Star-Eagle *(9/30/1935) reported that twenty thousand people participated in the procession of the Feast of Saint Michael in 1935.*
The angels pictured above are seven-year-old Julie Alfieri Venero and Barbara Onove West. They are suspended from ropes on opposite sides of Seventh Avenue near Sheffield Street.
(Photo: Julie Venero)

Procession in honor of Our Lady of Snows (Madonna della Neve), patroness of Calabritto, circa 1950. In Calabritto, the statue is carried from a chapel outside the town, and as it enters the town, it is greeted by a statue of Saint Joseph. The early Calabrittani who settled in the First Ward recreated this procession in Newark. Although the procession was discontinued long ago, Calabrittani still gather at Saint Lucy's each July for the panegirico *and sing the traditional* cantilene *(a slow, repetitive song) before the statue of Our Lady of Snows. They carry on a tradition established by the first Calabrittani who arrived here more than 120 years ago.* (Photo: Alex Zecca)

Feast of Saint Rocco on Sheffield Street, circa 1950. Saint Rocco's Feast and the Feast of Our Lady of the Assumption both took place in mid-August and were sometimes celebrated as a single grand feast with two bands outside the church. Saint Michael's Feast, which followed in September, featured an Italian mandolin band (mandolata). *A popular singer named Clara Stella (she was billed as the "Italian Mae West") performed at many of the feasts. In the evening the celebrations were capped off with fireworks staged near the railroad bridge at the top of the Sheffield Street hill.* (Photo: Fannie De Donna)

Quaint and unusual and of a traditional nature are the customs surrounding the annual festival in honor of Saint Gerardo. It is recognized as one of the most impressive celebrations of the year in the Italian neighborhood of the city. The twenty-fifth festival held recently was no exception to the rule of whole-hearted participation and colorful display. . . . Huge and elaborate candles are carried as an indication of humility and respect. Thousands march along, young and old, straight and supple, bent and fatigued, the latter of whom would follow until they fell from sheer exhaustion. Hundreds trudge on bare feet and from the windows eager, admiring faces look down as the saintly figure is showered with money.

—*Sunday Call* 11/2/1924

One faction of the Boyden Street Italians was celebrating Saint Rocco's Day. The day it appears is not of itself of much significance, but it was seized upon as an occasion on which the superior wealth and liberality of this faction might be flaunted in the faces of the members of the rival crowd. The latter have for their leader Gerardo Spatola, and the others for their leader Alfonso Ilaria, better known as King Alfonso. . . . Boyden Street, from Nassau Street to Eighth Avenue, was aglow with the light of hundreds of Chinese lanterns. A big platform had been erected over the door of King Alfonso's saloon and there were seated the musicians, resplendent in gay uniforms and surrounded by waving flags. At nightfall the band began to play and the red, green, and blue balls of fire began to ascend. Hundreds of people filled the street, and every minute brought more.

——*Newark Journal* 9/25/1891

Night scene during a feast at Saint Lucy's Church, circa 1958.
(Photo: Saint Lucy's Archives)

Cecere Family funeral on Stone Street, circa 1930.
(Photo: Spatola Family)

FUNERALS

First Ward funerals could be as spectacular and as emotion-laden as the feasts, at times rivaling them, as the corteges slowly wound their way through the neighborhood's narrow streets. A band often escorted the deceased from the wake to the church, followed by a long line of coaches filled with floral tributes from acquaintances and friends.

Wakes were held at the home of the deceased and black crepe or a swag over the doorway served as a sign of mourning. A white swag was sometimes substituted if the deceased was a child or young girl. Relatives, neighbors, and friends came to pay their respects, filling the house with mourners day and night. Failure to appear at the wake or to pay one's respects to the deceased and the bereaved family could lead to bad feelings among neighbors, which could persist for decades. Everyone attending the wake made a contribution to the *poste* to help defray the expense of the funeral. It was customary to write one's name and the amount one contributed in a book kept next to the poste box. Cooking was not permitted in the house during the period of grieving, and neighbors brought food for the bereaved family.

Wakes were sometimes quite eventful. Tenement stairwells were torturously steep and were quite narrow, presenting a formidable challenge when it was time to remove the body. During the wake held for a woman of considerable girth who occupied a top floor flat on Eighth Avenue, the problem was solved by removing the window frames and lowering the coffin into the street with a pulley. Another potential danger was the custom of continuously burning candles in the room where the body was displayed. Family members kept a close watch, but on one occasion, during the wake for Filomena Celentano, the coffin caught fire, causing quite an uproar. Richie Boiardo, who was present, rescued the body from the burning coffin.

Large funeral processions marked the passing of notable figures, such as Monsignor Perotti, slain police detective Tom Adubato, and gangland figures, such as Big Joe Giuliano (who died in the electric chair) and Frank Mazzocchi. On such occasions thousands of onlookers, many motivated by simple curiosity, turned out to gawk or to become part of the spectacle. But without question, the most unusual funeral the First Ward ever witnessed took place in 1920 when a cobbler named Emidio Russomanno held a funeral for his pet canary. He hired a fifteen-piece band, a hearse, and four pall bearers. Thousands of people gathered outside Russomanno's shop on Boyden Street on the day of the funeral and thousands more lined the streets to view the funeral procession.

Because customs associated with funerals were so ritualized, undertakers became important participants in the community. This was true at times of personal grieving, such as the unexpected death of a young child, but especially so

Detail of Cecere funeral. (Photo: Spatola Family)

Funeral of three-month-old Anna Nicastro on Drift Street in 1930.
(Photo: Dolores Nicastro)

during periods of grief which affected the entire neighborhood. For example, when the Spanish flu epidemic of 1918 claimed many lives, including numerous children, rows of pine coffins were stacked outside the undertakers' houses and funeral processions literally followed one upon the other along Seventh Avenue. The undertaker's function, paradoxically, was to cauterize the grief and at the same to choreograph the funeral in a way that was appropriately public.

Gerardo Spatola was one of the earliest Italian undertakers. Spatola was a barber in 1893 when he went to City Hall to a get a dog license but, as a result of a misunderstanding (Spatola spoke Italian), he was issued a livery permit instead. Since an undertaker needed little more than a horse, carriage, a container, and some ice, Spatola decided to try his hand at it. He became one of the first Italian funeral directors in New Jersey.

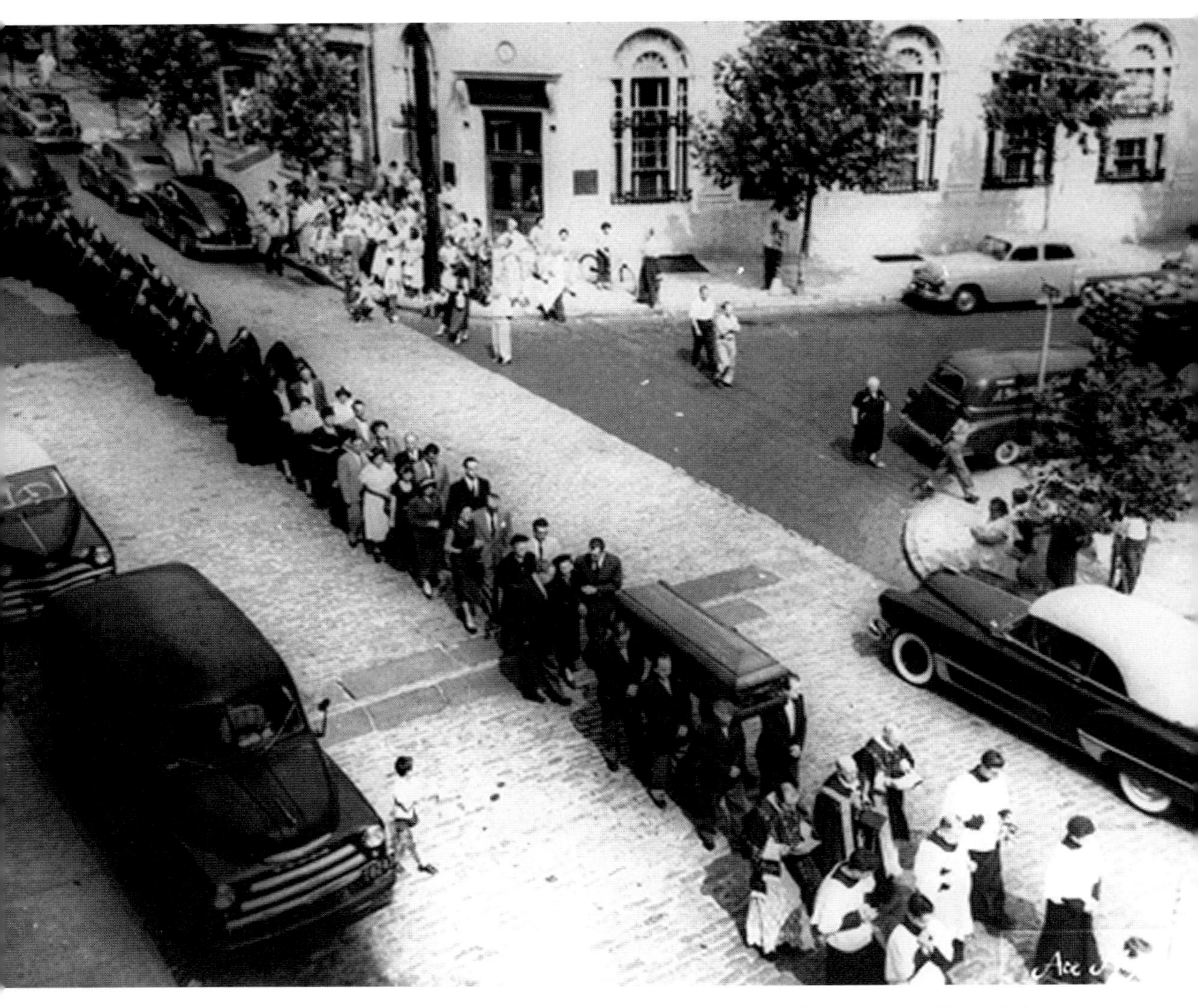

Funeral procession on Seventh Avenue for a deceased member of the Sisters of Saint John, circa 1947. (Photo: Ace Alagna)

Funeral procession on Garside Street near the corner of Seventh Avenue. The photograph, taken by Paolo Emilio De Rogatis, documents a double funeral held in 1931 for two ten-year-old boys. They lived in the same building and died when a backstop collapsed during a ball game at the Branch Brook Park reservoir. (Photo: Rose De Rogatis)

Funeral processions, such as the one depicted, left a lasting impression on children growing up in the neighborhood who were particularly impressed by the number of coaches filled with flowers. Italian girls skipped rope to a rhyme that went:

MOTHER, MOTHER, I AM SICK,
SEND FOR THE DOCTOR, QUICK, QUICK, QUICK,
DOCTOR, DOCTOR, WILL I DIE?
YES, MY CHILD, BUT DON'T YOU CRY.
HOW MANY COACHES WILL I HAVE?
ONE, TWO, THREE. . .

Even after death, the deceased were regarded as participating members of the family. Postmortem photographs were quite common and sometimes, especially if the deceased was an infant, were kept beside portraits of other family members. Photographer Rodolfo Colamedici produced postmortem portraits as well as medallions for gravestones. Colamedici used flash powder when photographing and once, when producing a postmortem of a shooting victim, he warned the family not to be alarmed by the loud noise from the powder. Sure enough, when the powder flashed the terrified family screamed and everyone ran for cover convinced that the murderer had returned to kill them all.

Burial plots at Holy Sepulcher Cemetery were lovingly maintained and were frequently visited. Graves were often adorned with statues of Saint Rocco, Saint Gerard, or Saint Sabino, and families who could afford it placed a life-size marble statue of the deceased at the grave. When Raffaele Nicastro died, his family sent his suit, shoes, hat, and photograph to Italy to have his statue produced. It was completed in 1938 but was rerouted so many times, because of the war, it did not arrive until five years later.

Postmortem photograph of three-month-old Anna Nicastro at her family's house on Drift Street in 1930. (Photo: Dolores Nicastro)

Family members gather at the grave of the Racioppi family at Holy Sepulcher Cemetery in 1930. Holy Sepulcher, where many First Ward families were buried, is about two miles from Saint Lucy's Church, and after the funeral mass family members often walked in procession all the way to the grave site. Pictured above are Pat De Rogatis, Rosuccia Racioppi De Rogatis, Gerald Rotonda, and Rose De Rogatis. (Photo: Rose De Rogatis)

The Canary Funeral

When Boyden Street cobbler Emidio Russomanno's pet canary died in 1920, apparently from swallowing a watermelon seed, Russomanno decided to hold a funeral. He went to the funeral director Gerardo Spatola, his lifelong friend, and asked him to make the appropriate arrangements. He hired a fifteen-piece band, a hearse, and two coaches, purchased a white coffin for twenty-five dollars, and engaged four pallbearers. Thousands of people gathered outside Russomanno's shop at 5 Boyden Street on the day of the funeral. The cobbler's shop was draped in black crepe and Jimmy, the canary, was laid out in a six-inch by twelve-inch coffin on the cobbler's workbench, surrounded by flowers, a crucifix, and six lighted candles. A phonograph played funeral music and every so often the band played a dirge. Thousands lined the streets and followed behind the funeral cortege. The *Star-Eagle* of August 4, 1920 reported, "The undertaker held his sides. The coach drivers had tears in their eyes from laughter. The pallbearers shook with merriment and almost upset the coffin. The members of the fifteen-piece band . . . chuckled as they played solemn dirges."

All the while Russomanno rode in a coach and between fits of weeping, muttered aloud: "Oh, what the hell. Jimmy's dead, I shouldn't cry anymore." Then he once more burst into tears. Newsreel cameramen were there to record the event. Just as the band began playing a dirge a fire broke out in a stable on D'Auria Street, one block away. The cameramen and part of the crowd rushed to observe the fire and then quickly returned. As the band played "Nearer My God to Thee," the strange procession made its way through Sheffield Street to Nassau Street, and along Eighth Avenue and Seventh Avenue. Crowds, estimated at as many as ten thousand, lined the streets, or watched from fire escapes, rooftops, and windows. The funeral cost 200 dollars and Russomanno's neighbors contributed 178 dollars to help pay for it.

Pallbearers carry "Jimmy's" casket.
(Photo: *Sunday Call* 8/15/1920)

Emidio Russomanno outside his cobbler's shop on Boyden Street during the funeral of his pet canary.
(Photo: Steve Longo)

A crowd gathers outside the cobbler's shop prior to canary funeral. (Photo: Steve Longo)

The funeral procession makes its way along Boyden Street.
(Photo: *Sunday Call* 8/15/1920)

Detective Tom Adubato. Adubato was the first Italian-American detective killed in the line of duty. He worked on nearly one hundred murder cases, and newspapers reported that at least a dozen of the men he apprehended "paid the penalty in the electric chair". (Photo: Gerry Pesci)

BLACKHANDERS, BOOTLEGGERS, SAINTS & SINNERS

At the beginning of the century, Newark's newspapers carried numerous accounts of Italians engaging in criminal behavior, wielding razors, pistols, and stilettos. These lurid tales helped inform and enliven the stereotype of the hot-blooded Italian. To their neighbors of mostly northern European ancestry, the southern Italians seemed especially foreign. Drift Street was considered particularly turbulent. Squalid conditions in crowded tenements of the Italian quarter were, in fact, breeding grounds for crime. Children were enlisted at an early age. A Fagin-type gang operated in the vicinity of Drift Street stealing bread and milk from the doorsteps. One gang, including a pair of six-year olds, was apprehended with a cache of "cheap jewelry, sleeve buttons, a razor, a pocketbook containing thirty-six cents and other small articles" (*Newark News*, May 12, 1903).

The first decade of the century witnessed the appearance of secret criminal societies, known as the Black Hand (*La Mano Nero*) and the Mafia. These were extortion rings that preyed upon Italian neighborhoods. Victims of the Black Hand received letters demanding a sum of money and a warning that harm would come to their person, property, or family should they fail to comply. The anonymity of the demand was perfectly suited to pranksters, freelance extortionists, shakedown artists, and almost anyone with a grudge. Following a spate of incidents in New York in 1903, the Black Hand made its appearance in Newark. Wealthy Italians were targeted, and a few prominent Italians were permitted to carry pistols for their own protection after receiving death threats. When some of the threats turned out to be hoaxes, the journal *La Frusta* scoffed: "If a cat turns up dead, there is a front-page story in a New York newspaper holding the Mafia responsible."

The era of the Black Hand produced an authentic hero in the person of Police Detective Thomas Adubato. Adubato stood well over six feet tall and sported a thick handlebar mustache. As the first Italian detective on the Newark police force, the task of investigating and solving Black Hand cases often fell to him. He was considered fearless and was credited with breaking up several gangs of blackhanders. Adubato's death was as heroic as his life. In the course of a murder investigation in 1918, Adubato pursued a suspect to a New York City tenement where he and a fellow officer were shot. Adubato managed to carry the other officer down five flights of stairs, but died himself several hours later.

A decade later the exploits of the Four Reid Bandits caught the imagination of the neighborhood. The gang drew its name from the robbery and murder of a payroll courier outside the Reid Ice Cream factory on Clay Street. Four men were charged with murder, including "Big Joe" Giuliano of Eighth Avenue and Nicolas Joseph "Little Joe" Giuliano of Aqueduct Alley. They became known as the Four Reid Bandits. All four were convicted and sentenced to die in the electric chair. Shortly after the trial, a key witness recanted. But their appeals were denied and they went to the chair in 1927 proclaiming their innocence. Big Joe's dying words were "They framed me. I'm innocent." Two days later the bodies of Big Joe and Little Joe Giuliano were brought home and displayed in bronze coffins. A crowd of more than three thousand gathered outside Big Joe's home on Eighth Avenue on the morning of the funeral. The execution of the Reid bandits, barely three months after the Sacco and Vanzetti executions, drew the attention of Italian newspapers as far away as the *Corriere de la Sera* of Milan, which protested: "Despite the doubts of the guilt of several Italians, the American machine of justice did not stop."

When Prohibition closed the saloons and the sale of liquor was outlawed, bootlegging became a lucrative business. Illegal stills and speakeasies proliferated in the First Ward, and in the late 1920s competition for control of the liquor and lottery trade erupted in violence. Rival gangs raided the neighborhood on numerous occasions, spraying the streets with bullets. The focus of several incidents was the American Victory Café, a Seventh Avenue speakeasy and headquarters of the Mazzocchi brothers. Several gangsters met their deaths on Seventh Avenue after visiting the Victory Café, including a reputedly "former lieutenant of Al Capone." Frank Mazzocchi, the self-styled "Rum King of the First Ward," was murdered outside the club in 1930. He died in a hail of bullets fired from a passing sedan.

Ruggiero Boiardo—known later in his career as "Richie the Boot"—was the most famous First Ward figure of the Prohibition era. Boiardo came to Newark from Chicago in 1910. For a time he drove a milk truck on Boyden Street. Eventually he gained a foothold in the lottery and bootlegging rackets using the name "Ritchie." He became a larger than life figure sporting a five-thousand-dollar diamond-studded belt buckle, and local newspaper accounts of his exploits ("Ritchie's Fabled Belt Buckle Sign of Rule in Brooklyn, Too" and "Power of Ritchie in Rackets Strong") added to his stature. Boiardo's influence in the First Ward was so great that politicians openly courted him and he was considered a kingmaker.

Boiardo's principal rival was Abner "Longey" Zwillman, who controlled the rackets in Newark's Third Ward Jewish quarter but also had a foothold in the First Ward. Newark had become an important East Coast bootlegging center, the headquarters of the "Reinfeld Syndicate" which emerged from Joe Reinfeld's First Ward saloon. At Reinfeld's saloon Italian and Jewish racketeers hobnobbed with local politicians. Reinfeld used his political connections and his link to the Canadian distiller Sam Bronfman to ship Canadian liquor into Port Newark. Zwillman became Reinfeld's protégé and eventually emerged as a major underworld figure in partnership with Lucky Luciano and Meyer Lansky. He reputedly helped engineer the murder of Dutch Shultz in Newark and then absorbed some of the Dutchman's operation. He also carried on a long relationship with the actress Jean Harlow.

The so-called Ritchie/Longey feud erupted in 1930 over control of the city's bootlegging and lottery rackets. The rival gangs plundered each other's territory; however, subsequent raids by the police against both factions led them to seek a truce. Boiardo staged a two-day dinner in his own honor at a Seventh Avenue restaurant to which Zwillman was invited. The dinner, attended by scores of politicians and underworld figures, captured the attention of the local papers. The two gang leaders shook hands and a truce was declared. Less than two months later Boiardo was ambushed on North Broad Street. The attack was apparently unconnected to the feud with Longey's gang. Boiardo was rushed to a hospital with more than a dozen shotgun slugs in his body. He survived but was charged with carrying concealed weapons and was sentenced to two and a half years in prison.

After his release from prison, Boiardo built the Vittorio Castle restaurant and banquet hall on Eighth Avenue. The Castle became a First Ward magnet, attracting celebrities, politicians, and underworld figures. Boiardo's son, Anthony ("Tony Boy") Boiardo, managed the Castle for his father who could not hold a liquor license, and was often described as the elder Boiardo's "right hand man." In 1950 more than fifteen thousand people filled Sheffield Street to view the bride and groom when Tony Boy was married at Saint Lucy's Church.

By the 1950s Boiardo had "retired" to a thirty-room mansion in Livingston,

New Jersey. He kept a low profile until 1963, when Joe Valachi fingered him as a *capo* (captain) in the Genovese crime family, a charge he denied before a grand jury. In 1969 he was convicted of gambling conspiracy. In 1979, at the age of eighty-eight, he was indicted on charges of racketeering and murder conspiracy in the so-called "Great Mob Trial" which, for the first time, sought to establish the existence of *La Cosa Nostra*. Boiardo was eventually severed from the case because of failing health. He died on October 29, 1984, at the age of ninety-three.

Despite his reputation as an underworld figure, Boiardo was much admired and respected in the First Ward. His standing as a "philanthropist" was established early in his career, and by 1930 it was said that "whole families in the First Ward fall back on him in their times of need." In his later years, he was even regarded as a kind of patriarch in the First Ward, a wise elder statesman referred to with deference as the "old man," whose advice was often solicited. Rightly or wrongly, many First Warders considered him a patron and benefactor, and a protector of the neighborhood.

Richie Boiardo, photographed during a banquet held in his honor. The "Boot" was a larger than life figure in the First Ward and accounts of his exploits often blend fact with fiction. It was alleged that during his feud with Longey Zwillman, he dispatched two men dressed in women's clothes to dispose of his foe. Others tell of the time when Al Capone stopped by the Victory Cafe to pay his respects. At first a Boiardo lieutenant didn't recognize Capone. "He's not here," he snapped at the gangster from Chicago. "Tell him Al Capone stopped by," Capone replied. Boiardo's man apologized nervously and hurried off to find the Boot. Boiardo was said to sometimes pay associates with barrels of silver dollars, his personal trademark. Boiardo's fortress-like estate in Livingston, New Jersey, was the subject of a Life *magazine photo spread.*
(Photo: *Star-Eagle* 10/7/1930)

Notorious Aqueduct Alley, looking east from Clifton Avenue, circa 1915. Aqueduct Alley ran just a single block downhill from Clifton Avenue to a little bend, where it exited into Eighth Avenue. There was always a dice game running in Aqueduct Alley. Neighborhood toughs kept a lookout at the top of the hill on Clifton Avenue near Eighth Avenue. They would holler out a warning or whistle an alarm whenever the police approached to break up the game. An easy escape was through the backyards of the tenements along Factory Street where the overhanging laundry provided a dense cover. In the evenings, they rolled their dice by candlelight. Occasionally police raided a nearby cafe or pool parlor with gambling tables or an illegal game of ziconette. The lookout's warning call would send the players tumbling out a doorway or a window, with the police in hot pursuit. Drift Street, one block away, also gained a kind of notoriety. Big Joe and Little Joe Giuliano frequented Jilly Grande's pool hall on Drift Street. (Photo: Newark Public Library)

Richie Boiardo photographed in 1979, at age eighty-eight, outside the Somerset County Court House before being severed from the so-called Great Mob Trial.
(Photo: New Jersey Newsphotos)

Ritchie, as he is known to his henchmen, is a big man, immaculately attired and wears a monstrous diamond belt buckle. This buckle, says Ritchie, is valued intrinsically at $5,000 in cash, but is worth much more to him, as it was the means of saving his life in approved movie manner. It once stopped a bullet intended for the big boy's innards. He also wears a scarf pin heavily encrusted with diamonds and a ring that looks like a baby spotlight used in theaters.

—*Newark News* 10/6/1930

Abner "Longey" Zwillman (foreground, left) and Jerry Catena (right) at Vittorio Castle. Faced with a conviction for income tax evasion, Zwillman committed suicide in 1959.
(Photo: From *Gangster #2*, by Mark Stuart)

Marconi Tavern at 181 Eighth Avenue in 1938. The owner Dominick Fiorello poses with his sons, Sam and Tony, behind the bar. (Photo: Philip Gentile)

THE WARD

The evolution from immigrant enclave to Italian-American neighborhood was a slow and complex process, and during the 1930s the First Ward underwent yet another transformation. "Little Italy" was becoming "The Ward" but without entirely sacrificing its old-world charm. Those who grew up in the First Ward during this period recall it with fondness, despite the hard times, as a place where everyone knew one other. It was a place where old people were respectfully called "z'Emidio" (uncle) and "comar'Rosa" (godmother), and it was safe to walk the streets late in the evening because the young men who gathered outside their clubhouses knew each other's families and felt honor-bound to look out for each other's sisters, aunts, or cousins. The barbershop, the grocery store, the butchershop, the streetcorner, and the stoop, all became social centers because the flats where people lived were small and crowded. Taverns, such as Marconi's and Gabriello's, had a "family room" and were always packed on a Saturday night when patrons dined for free on tripe and capozzelle.

A new generation of storefront social clubs, with names like Abadaba Klub, Annatoles Pleasure Club, Ackwees Athletic Club, and Klub Avalon, now lined the neighborhood streets. Older clubs, such as Circolo Progressista Caposelese and Circolo Atripaldese, preserved an old-world flavor, while the second generation clubs held outings, boat rides, and dances.

On Sundays and summer evenings, families gathered in Branch Brook Park for picnics and band concerts or strolled through the Italian Gardens. Grandfathers tended backyard gardens or passed the time playing bocce. There were numerous bocce alleys scattered about the neighborhood, including official clubs, such as the Victory Club on Eighth Avenue, public courts on D'Auria Street and in Branch Brook Park, and countless backyard alleys. The Ward had a single small movie house, the Colonial, where the band leader Ted Fio Rito occasionally played the piano. During the 1930s, the First Ward often "went to the movies" at the McKinley School playground on Eighth Avenue. The movies, sponsored by the city of Newark, were projected onto an outside wall of the school. Entire families attended and sometimes brought their suppers. Dances, theatrical productions, sporting events, and band competitions were held at the Italian Catholic Union, a three-story building at the corner of Summer Avenue and D'Auria Street. It had a gymnasium, an auditorium, bowling alleys, and a bocce court. Dances with live bands were held twice a week at the ICU. Admission was twenty-five cents and local musicians had an opportunity to perform, among them a skinny teenager from Hoboken, named Frank Sinatra, who once had to be chased from the stage by a burly trombone player because he wouldn't stop singing. The ICU had about 1,200 members and was the largest association in the First Ward. Its members included lawyers, doctors, teachers, and blue collar workers.

Outside the Ward, Italian operas and concerts were staged by the impresario Alfredo Cerrigone at the Newark Opera House on Washington Avenue; Italian-language films were screened at several Newark movie houses, including the Little Theater on Broad Street; and live performances by popular Italian entertainers were aired on radio station WNJ which broadcast Ben D'Avella's "An Evening in Naples" from the Hotel Saint Francis on Park Street. Rallies and large political gatherings were organized at the nearby City Armory on Sussex Avenue.

The focal point of the neighborhood, however, was Sheffield Street, between Seventh and Eighth Avenue, the site of Saint Lucy's Church. On Sunday mornings, music from Antonio Caprio's music store (Libreria Figlia D'Italia) serenaded people on their way to mass or shopping for the Sunday meal. Sheffield Street had several bakeries and markets, including Salvatore Palumbo's Fish Market. At Christmas, Palumbo placed a rowboat outside his shop and decorated its mast with Italian and American flags. The boat was filled with live eels, a delicacy favored by Italians at Christmas. A barker stood in the doorway shouting "U capadone, u capadone. Vive e grosso." (Eels, eels! Live and big!). Sheffield Street had a famous pork store noted for the sobriquet of the proprietor's wife—"Sangue di Montagna" (blood of the mountain). However, it was during the feasts that Sheffield Street came truly alive. A sea of lights illuminated the bandstands, the rows of food stalls, and the people dancing in the street to the tunes of popular Italian songs and operas that filled the air.

Seventh Avenue, the neighborhood's second most important artery, ran eight short blocks downhill from Clifton Avenue to Belleville Avenue. The Essex County Brewery once dominated the corner of Seventh Avenue and Clifton Avenue until it closed during Prohibition. Seventh Avenue School (renamed McKinley School) occupied the block between Factory Street and Amity Place, where it faced the old Saint Lucy's rectory. The Second Police Precinct stood at the corner of Seventh Avenue and Summer Avenue. Three Italian-owned banks were located on Seventh Avenue as well as the Italian Protestant Church and numerous Italian markets and specialty shops. As many as twenty social clubs and nine Italian bakeries and pastry shops lined Seventh Avenue. Several Jewish merchants also had shops on Seventh Avenue, including Philip Meyer, who spoke Italian "better than most of his customers." There was also Abraham Bienstock, who had a long, red beard and was called "Old Fox in the Bush" by the Italian children.

Eighth Avenue, from the Clifton Avenue entrance of Branch Brook Park all the way to John Street, was the colorful heart of Newark's Little Italy. From its earliest days, it was the district's principal thoroughfare. Scores of Italian fraternal societies had their headquarters there. Political meetings and social gatherings were held at its meeting halls. Thousands gathered here for the grand feasts at Saint Lucy's Church when the avenue was ablaze with decorative lights. The Italian presence along Eighth Avenue lasted about seventy-five years, from 1880 to 1955. Originally called Quarry Street, it was once an Irish stronghold; by 1900 it was practically all Italian. Italians built most of the buildings that defined the Avenue during the first half of the century. The Italian period, though relatively brief, was tumultuous, spanning two world wars, Prohibition, and the Great Depression. In the course of these years the Avenue, reflecting the steady evolution of the entire enclave, was transformed from an old-world Little Italy to a bustling Italian-American thoroughfare.

By 1940 Eighth Avenue had become the First Ward's restaurant row. "On a Saturday night, Eighth Avenue rivaled Little Italy in New York," a former First Warder recalls. Just about everyone came to the Ward. Crowds outside the Vittorio Castle craned for a glimpse of Joe DiMaggio, boxing legends Joe Louis and Jack Dempsey, actor George Raft, and other celebrities who came from New York to dine on Eighth Avenue. Eighth Avenue's restaurants varied in size. Some were strictly neighborhood places, such as Cilio's and Big Mike's. Others, like Vittorio Castle, Vesuvius, Alfano's, and La Casa attracted a mixed crowd. The Vittorio Castle Banquet Hall, at the corner of Summer Avenue and Eighth Avenue, was the most elaborate restaurant in the area. Built by Ruggerio Boiardo and his associates during the early 1930s, it was adorned with turrets and towers. The Castle became a First Ward landmark. "The Boot" held court there and a steady procession of politicians, celebrities, and gangland figures came to the

Castle to wine and dine. Vesuvius Restaurant, at the corner of Sheffield Street and Eighth Avenue, had an open-air summer garden and was perhaps the finest restaurant on the Avenue.

Sardella's restaurant on Sheffield Street was a popular First Ward "after-hours joint." At Sardella's, gangsters hobnobbed with musicians, actors, and showgirls. The big bands played Newark's theaters in those days, and Sardella's was the place they came to after the show. The food was terrific, the liquor flowed, and it was open all night. There was a narrow alley nearby and if the police arrived, it was easy to slip out. Musicians "felt right at home," explained a former waitress, and they came night after night. Tommy and Jimmy Dorsey, Guy Lombardo, Benny Goodman, Harry James, Louie Prima, Doris Day, and Carole Lombard were part of Sardella's crowd. Jess D. Myers, owner of Newark's big burlesque house, the Empire Theater, brought his showgirls, among them the stripper Gypsy Rose Lee. Billie Holiday once emerged from Sardella's dragging her sable coat in the snow. A fan called out, "What did you eat, Billie?" "Linguini with clam sauce!" the singer called back.

The nightly scene at Sardella's reflected the new currents in the neighborhood and was a harbinger of things to come. The Ward was changing. From the clubhouses, the flats, and the fire escapes, the sound of big band music now competed with the arias and Neapolitan melodies heard on the popular radio program "An Evening in Naples." And for a second time, a generation of First Warders was preparing to go off to war.

Italian Catholic Union Building (Photo: Saint Lucy's Archives)

Family room at Marconi Tavern on a Saturday evening. On Saturday night, taverns provided free food and free music for their patrons. Besides tripe and capozzelle *(sheep's head), the menu included* saracca *(salted herring),* soffrite *(stewed lungs in a red sauce),* shushelle *(a long bean with a licorice taste), hard-boiled eggs, and falva beans. This salty fare whetted the thirst so that patrons drank lots of beer. Neighborhood taverns only served beer and Wilson's whiskey, as families generally produced their own brandy and anisette. At one time, a pail of beer at Luigi Papara's Saloon on Seventh Avenue or Cici Paolo's place on Garside Street cost about twenty-five cents.* (Photo: Philip Gentile)

Ralph Russomanno, standing at left, in his barber shop at the corner of High Street and Summer Avenue. (Photo: Jerry Russomanno)

Neighborhood clubs sprang up at every corner of the First Ward. There were first generation mutual aid societies, old guard clubs such as *Dopo Lavora* (After-Work Club), which openly supported Mussolini, political clubs such as the Fred Hartley Republican Club and the First Ward Democratic Club, storefront "pleasure clubs," and athletic clubs. Men gathered at the clubs to talk, play cards, and sip coffee. Since there were no neighborhood cafés in those days, clubs had their own espresso machines. During the 1930s and 1940s, the proliferation of second generation clubs, which held dances and outings, contributed to the social cohesion of the neighborhood. The clubs sponsored ball teams and competed against each other. Teams in the First Ward Softball League played in an abandoned reservoir in Branch Brook Park.

Members of the First Ward Democratic Club at 205 Eighth Avenue, photographed in 1933. Shown from the left are Phil Giordano, Jerry Conforti, Al Farese, Joseph Tuozzolo, John Mascellino, and Ben Carnivale in foreground. (Photo: Palmina Mascellino)

Members of the Ackwees Club pose outside their club house on Eighth Avenue in 1934. The club was located near Aqueduct Alley, from which it derived its name. (Photo: Alfred Nittoli)

Members of the Ackwees ball team pose outside their club house. (Photo: Alfred Nittoli)

Members of the Societa Santa S. F. Cabrini, circa 1940, photographed at Masi Hall on Eighth Avenue. (Photo: Rita Masi)

Victory Bocce Club on Eighth Avenue, circa 1936. (Photo: Newark Public Library)

Armando Cilento and Angelo Salvatore outside a pork store on Sheffield Street in 1932.
(Photo: Armando Cilento)

First Ward bakery shops and pastry shops were legendary. At one time there were forty-two Italian bakers active in the neighborhood and every one managed to make a living. Italian pastry shops (*pasticerria*) such as Ferrara's, Boscia's, and Castellano's, specialized in sweet pastry or *dolci*. Other bakers were known for their round loaf (*panelle*), their *tarrales* (hard Italian pretzels) or their pizza loaf. Bakers prepared special products for holidays such as Christmas and Easter. At Christmas, they made panettone and holiday tarrales. For Easter they made *pane-grande* (a grain pie) and *u cassadelle* (a sweet bread), which was sometimes made in the form of an Easter basket.

Theresa Quatrucci, known as "La Signora," proprietor of the Tripoli Pasticerria at 23 Sheffield Street, peers through the window of her establishment, circa 1930. The lamb in window suggests that the photo was taken during Easter. (Photo: Theresa Colamedici)

The Giordano family poses outside Stefano Giordano's bakery at 33 Seventh Avenue in 1939. It was established in 1913. Stefano Giordano owned a flour mill in Caserta, near Naples. During a worldwide depression in the late 1880s, he emigrated to Newark with his brothers Modesto, Nicolo, and Tony. Three of the brothers established bakeries in the First Ward. Giordano's, operated by Stefano's grandson, was the last surviving First Ward bakery. Some years ago Frank Sinatra tasted Giordano's bread and since then has had it flown to his Palms Springs home, sometimes fifty loaves at a time. (Photo: James Procopio)

The Arre children, Marie, Peter, Nancy, and Theresa, pose outside the family's bakery shop at 63 Summer Avenue in 1936.
(Photo: Theresa Racanelli)

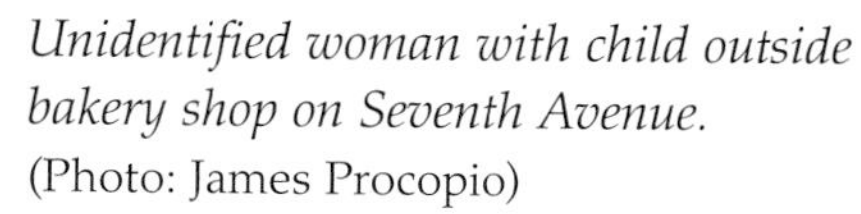

Unidentified woman with child outside bakery shop on Seventh Avenue.
(Photo: James Procopio)

The First Ward restaurants, clam bars, and specialty shops lured a steady stream of celebrities to Eighth Avenue. Joe DiMaggio, Jack Dempsey, the Dorsey Brothers, and George Raft came nightly, and kids lined up outside the Castle to collect autographs or to tug at the sleeve of Jimmy Durante, Rocky Marchiano, or Abbot and Costello. One witness recalled Marilyn Monroe arriving late one evening in a limousine. The crowd in the street grew so big she had to flee. "I guess she was looking for Joe," he surmised. Over the years, nightspots, such as Vesuvius, the Grotto, Twenty-Two, and the Sorrento Restaurant, attracted everyone from Jackie Gleason to Jayne Mansfield. They came not simply for the food, but also because of the neighborhood's appealing atmosphere, a mixture of old-world Italian provincialism with a tough 1930s American edge. It was neither too sophisticated nor too naive. Both gangsters and gumshoes felt at home here. The presence of movie actors, sports figures, and musicians added an air of excitement to Eighth Avenue and was a source of great pride for those who grew up in the Ward.

Members of the Siciliano family, owners of Vesuvius Restaurant, pose behind the restaurant's bar. Landmark First Ward restaurants, such as Vesuvius, Bill's Clam Bar, and Nanina's, began as fish markets. On weekends they would put out a few tables and provide a clam bar. Eventually people were lining up outside waiting to get in. (Photo: *Italian Tribune*)

Rose and Babe Tubello and friends at Vittorio Castle. (Photo: Mildred Avitable)

Banquet at Vittorio Castle. Anthony ("Tony Boy") Boiardo is seated in the foreground at the extreme right. Richie Boiardo is just barely visible in the doorway at the far left. (Photo: Mildred Avitable)

Joe DiMaggio sits with Richie Boiardo at Vittorio Castle in 1939. Standing behind them are Anthony "Tony Boy" Boiardo (at right) and Jerry Spatola. As soon as word spread that "Joe D" was at the Castle or at Vesuvius, crowds gathered outside. DiMaggio's impact during the 1930s and 1940s can hardly be overstated. To have "Joe D" visit your neighborhood, especially an Italian-American neighborhood, was, as one First Warder said, "the greatest feeling in the world. The neighborhood idolized him." When Yankee games were broadcast, every radio in the First Ward was tuned in, and if DiMaggio hit a home run, a roar went up and people ran out into the street and cheered. DiMaggio often brought along some of his teammates, such as Joe Page, Yogi Berra, and Phil Rizzuto, as well as Yankee sportscaster Mel Allen. Occasionally he would pay an impromptu visit to a neighborhood club or bocce court. DiMaggio's engagement party to actress Dorothy Arnold was held at the Castle. (Photo: Spatola Family)

Boxer Tony Galento poses in front of Vittorio Castle restaurant at the corner of Eighth Avenue and Summer Avenue. (Photo: Spatola Family)

Florence and Lydia Tedesco with Tessie De Lauro, photographed on Cutler Street in 1944.
(Photo: Tina Tedesco)

Men outside Spatola Association headquarters on Eighth Avenue in 1937.
(Photo: Elaine Holenko)

Alfred Hitchcock, filming on John Street. In December 1943, Alfred Hitchcock came to the First Ward to shoot a scene for his film Shadow of a Doubt. *The British film director set up his camera on John Street, just one block from the historic Plume House, the rectory of the House of Prayer Church where the Reverend Hannibal Goodwin invented the first celluloid film in 1887.* (Photo: William Vandervert, *Life* Magazine, copyright Time Inc.)

Men pose with a young boy outside the Royal Nuts club house on Seventh Avenue during World War II. The window is decorated with a memorial display for club member. (Photo: Zarro Family)

MUSSOLINI

Mussolini's rise to power elicited great enthusiasm in the First Ward. Black Shirt parades were staged by patriotic Italian clubs to commemorate Italy's victories in Ethiopia. The *Italian Tribune* published messages from Il Duce and announced each victory with a bold headline. Fund drives were organized to benefit the Italian Red Cross when sanctions were imposed against Italy in 1935. Many Italian women contributed their rings and jewelry during a rally at the Newark Armory. Spontaneous celebrations erupted in 1936 when Mussolini announced the fall of Addis Ababa. Father Ruggiero rang the bells at Saint Lucy's Church for a full half hour and tearful parishioners crowded into the church for prayers of thanksgiving. The Italian vice consul delivered an emotional speech to several hundred Italian war veterans gathered on Bloomfield Avenue. More than two thousand people, many carrying burning torches, paraded through the streets. At nightfall, hundreds more converged at the Circolo Atripaldese on Eighth Avenue. A band played and fireworks lit up the sky. Several days later, a victory parade hailed Mussolini's conquest. A crowd gathered on Eighth Avenue and at the sound of a trumpet the roar "Ethiopia is Italian!" went up. Singing the fascist anthem, "Giovinezza," they marched through the streets led by a band. Children from Saint Lucy's School marched in step, dressed in black shirts, white blouses, and red silk neckerchiefs. World fencing champion Gerardo Cetrulo led one contingent. Cetrulo, who had been Rudolph Valentino's fencing instructor, wore a black shirt, khaki trousers, and a white fez. Along Seventh Avenue, he observed a white horse beside a policeman. At the spur of the moment, he seized the reins, commandeered the horse, and rode it at the head of the parade, waving his arm in Mussolini's fascist salute. Support for Mussolini faded almost overnight when Japan attacked Pearl Harbor and the United States entered the war against the Axis Powers.

Tom and Sam Zarro photographed on Seventh Avenue, circa 1943.
(Photo: Zarro Family)

A group of inductees, parading up Seventh Avenue near the corner of Garside Street, circa 1943.
(Photo: Armando Cilento)

Members of the Webster Athletic Association pose outside their club house on Webster Street, circa 1940. (Photo: James Procopio)

Neighbors on Mount Prospect Avenue celebrate the end of World War II.
(Photo: Annette Zarro Cifalino)

Celebrating the announcement of the end of World War II on August 15, 1945, residents of Mount Prospect Avenue hoist an effigy of Emperor Hirohito from a telephone pole.
(Photo: Annette Zarro Cifalino)

Congressman Peter Rodino photographed during the feast of Saint Gerard in 1950. Rodino was born on Factory Street and grew up on Seventh Avenue across from McKinley School. Later he lived at the corner of Drift Street and Clifton Avenue. His mother died when he was four, and he was raised by his father and stepmother. He once dreamed of a career as a writer and produced a novella titled Up Drift Street *(the manuscript was lost when he went into the service). He was elected to Congress in 1948. During his forty-year tenure in Congress, he sponsored major legislation promoting civil rights and voting rights, and fought to eliminate immigration quotas. He served for many years as chairman of the House Judiciary Committee, and in that capacity, presided over the committee's historic vote to impeach President Richard Nixon. Rodino remembers the First Ward as a place imbued with a "kindred feeling, almost akin to a family." "We grew up with a certain loyalty," he explained. "To recall that, gives me strength."*
(Photo: Tubello Family)

DISPLACEMENT

When World War II ended, the First Ward experienced a return to prosperity. Eighth Avenue was alive with activity. The feasts were as elaborate and boisterous as ever. New restaurants opened for business and on weekends people stood in line outside the Grotto, Sam Brown's Clam Bar, and Nanina Mari's Seafood Restaurant. But the postwar prosperity was in many ways deceptive. The neighborhood was showing signs of change. The immigrant generation was passing away and the neighborhood had become more Americanized. The old, crowded tenements, which always lacked central heating, private baths, and other amenities, had deteriorated with age. Young men, back from military service and about to start families, sought better quarters outside the Ward. Still, the neighborhood retained its Italian-American character. Many who moved away returned to visit their families, to frequent the social clubs, and to patronize the Italian specialty shops on Eighth Avenue and Seventh Avenue. They remained loyal to Saint Lucy's Church. Few First Warders foresaw the social forces that were about to overtake the neighborhood.

As early as the 1930s urban planners had begun to envision large-scale, federally funded urban redevelopment projects to restore blighted city neighborhoods. Planning was interrupted by the war, but by the late 1940s, federal legislation was in place and the first sites for renewal were chosen. The First

Ward contained some of the oldest housing stock in Newark and for years it had been promoted as a redevelopment site. Nevertheless, First Warders were shocked by the announcement in January 1952 that a large tract in the heart of the neighborhood had been selected for urban renewal. "Big Newark Slum To Be Housing Site!" declared the *New York Times* (June 14, 1952), which labeled the forty-million-dollar urban renewal plan "the largest slum clearance and development project in New Jersey."

The redevelopment area stretched from Clifton Avenue to Broad Street, and from Seventh Avenue to State Street. It covered 46 acres and had the highest housing density of any district in the city. Almost every building in the redevelopment zone (about 470 structures) would eventually be razed, replaced with eight twelve-story, low-income apartment buildings—the Columbus Homes—at the center of the tract, and three privately funded middle-income high-rise apartment buildings at the Clifton Avenue and Broad Street ends. Saint Lucy's Church, its parish hall, convent, and school, together with McKinley School, were among the few structures that were spared. About 4,600 people (1,300 families) were eventually displaced and Eighth Avenue, the First Ward's main artery, was leveled.

The redevelopment plan was supported by most of the leading figures in Newark's Italian-American community, among them Mayor Ralph Villani and Congressman Peter Rodino. Rodino was born in the First Ward and had grown up on Seventh Avenue. He was acquainted firsthand with the condition of the tenements and became an early champion of urban renewal. "I felt we could improve," said Rodino. "We visualized people coming into quarters that were up-to-date. The original design for Columbus Homes looked like a dream to me." But the decision to proceed with the project lay with city officials, and Mayor Villani took the lead. Villani had to contend with opposition from many First Warders who bitterly opposed the plan. Hundreds signed protest petitions. The "Save Our Homes Council" was formed and a lawsuit was filed to block the project. Mayor Villani met with residents who worried that the low-income ceilings would exclude them from the new housing. Villani, his voice full of emotion, asserted: "May God strike me dead if I want to harm anyone. Nobody will be thrown out into the streets. Some day you people will build a monument to me for what I'm trying to do for this city."

The Reverend Gaetano Ruggiero, pastor of Saint Lucy's Church, was among those who gave their support to the project. His successor, Monsignor Joseph Granato, believes Ruggiero did not grasp the scale of the project until it was too late. "He was sold a bill of goods," says Granato. "He thought the people could stay and have better homes. By the time he fully understood the enormity of the project, it was too late. When he saw that people were thrown out against their will, unable to return, he couldn't sleep for three years."

The gutting of the neighborhood began in July 1953, and it proceeded through several phases over the next three years. One by one the little streets surrounding Saint Lucy's Church began to disappear. D'Auria Street, Boyden Street, Drift Street, and Aqueduct Alley were leveled. Uprooted families felt profound grief, as if mourning a loved one who had passed away too soon. As one put it, "When they built Columbus Homes, they tore us apart." Said another, "It was a disaster. It broke people's hearts." Many felt betrayed. "It wasn't a choice," said one. "You had to get out." "They told us our homes were slums," said another, "they weren't slums." Many of the displaced had lived in the same building all their lives. Families were torn apart. Grandparents, aunts, and uncles who lived together under the same roof suddenly had to find new homes. Scores of family-owned businesses that thrived in the neighborhood were forced out and very few ever reopened. Properties were condemned and although the owners received compensation, it hardly mattered. Hardest hit were the elderly who had lived their entire lives amid family and neighbors and within walking distance of the church. They could not imagine living anywhere else. Some died as a result. "They were heartbroken," a former resident recalls. "A few months later you read their names in the obituaries." To this day, First Warders recall this period of dispersal with a feeling of sadness, bitterness, and betrayal. "We knew that it would never be the same," said one. "Everything came to an end."

On August 1, 1955, the Christopher Columbus Homes officially opened, but few displaced First Warders came back to live there. Nonetheless, the neighborhood sought to coexist with the new housing complex and Italian families occupied some of the apartments. The Reverend Ruggiero conducted a census of the buildings in an effort to incorporate the new families into the parish. Two years later, he built a new community center on Seventh Avenue. But in the end, the scale of the buildings overwhelmed what was left of the old neighborhood. Rather than stabilize the community, urban renewal hastened its deterioration. As one First Warder put it, "Those projects killed the Ward. It was over after that." Another First Warder, commenting on the project's size, put it even more bluntly: "They built monsters down there."

The coming of Columbus Homes marked the beginning of a long, torturous decline from which the First Ward never rebounded. While playing a significant part, the public housing complex was by no means the only factor that led to the neighborhood's decline. Newark, like other large urban centers, began to experience an erosion in its population as well as in its manufacturing base. The city's shrinking tax base, coupled with an increasingly indigent population, created a stress in the social fabric that adversely affected Newark's diverse neighborhoods. In 1967 the city was rocked by civil disturbances. In 1970 it was further polarized by a corruption scandal that eventually unseated the city's Italian-American mayor, Hugh J. Addonizio. At the same time, the death of the Reverend Ruggiero in 1966 deprived the First Ward of its spiritual leader. Monsignor Granato, who succeeded Ruggiero as pastor of Saint Lucy's in 1971, remembers this as "a period of five sad years over which we had virtually no influence and absolutely no control." By 1975 all that remained of the Italian First Ward were portions of Garside Street, Mount Prospect Avenue, Cutler Street, and Summer Avenue. By decade's end, the obliteration of the neighborhood was all but complete. It was an unnatural landscape, ravaged by years of decay, arson, vandalism, and neglect. Not a single structure remained standing north of Seventh Avenue along Wood Street, Stone Street, Cutler Street, and Crane Street, a barren three square blocks. Not a single soul resided in Columbus Homes. The eight buildings, each twelve stories tall, were partially closed in 1972, and then fully depopulated and boarded up in 1990. All that remained of the Italian neighborhood in the First Ward was Saint Lucy's Church.

Newark Mayor Ralph Villani cuts an eight-foot-long provolone weighing more than 600 pounds, displayed at Michael Galeotafiore's grocery store at 223 Eighth Avenue, in 1950.
(Photo: Newark Public Library)

Starting line during soap box derby on Sheffield Street, at corner of Nassau Street in 1949. Newark Mayor Ralph Villani is at left with hand raised. Congressman Peter Rodino is at center. (Photo: Caputo Family)

Float for 1945 Columbus Day parade, photographed at the corner of Eighth Avenue and Sheffield Street. Vesuvius Restaurant is at the opposite corner. (Photo: Caputo Family)

Members of Maddalonesi Society pose with statue of Saint Michael, circa 1947. (Photo: Suppa Family)

Procession for the Feast of Saint Rocco, circa 1945. (Photo: Paradiso Family)

Lillian Luciano, photographed on Eighth Avenue below Sheffield Street, circa 1948. (Photo: Lucille Vitale)

Bridal party of Angelina Suppa, daughter of Michael and Maria Suppa (at left), outside Suppa's Tavern at 171 Eighth Avenue, circa 1950. (Photo: Nick Graziano)

Children playing on Mount Prospect Avenue, circa 1948.
(Photo: Annette Zarro Cifalino)

"U Fumo"

Francesco Galleto was the famous First Ward sweet potato man known as "U Fumo." In the winter he sold chestnuts and hot sweet potatoes outside McKinley Elementary School, at the corner of Seventh Avenue and Factory Street. He had a little pushcart with a stove and three metal drawers on which he cooked his sweet potatoes. Great clouds of smoke (*fumo*) curled up from his oven and encircled him as he went about his work. U Fumo was tall and skinny with big ears and a big nose, and wore an oversized Italian army coat. He attracted customers by playing a funeral dirge on his bugle and ringing a bell, calling out, "Minialla, calda, calda!" (hot little balls). The children who gathered around him called him "Caldi-Cald." U Fumo's hands were "as black as coal" from handling the skins of his sweet potatoes, but everyone loved the way those potatoes tasted. Some considered him the last of the old-time street peddlers. He died in 1963.

Peddler Giro Caruso with son Vincent, circa 1945. (Photo: Vincent Caruso)

VIEWS OF FACTORY (BELOW) STREET AND EIGHTH AVENUE SHORTLY BEFORE THEY WERE LEVELED BY URBAN RENEWAL.

Factory Street, facing north toward Garside Street, circa 1948.
(Photo: Newark Public Library)

Eighth Avenue below Nesbitt Street, looking east, photographed in 1953.
(Photo: Anthony Megaro)

A drastic change in their mode of life is in prospect for First Ward residents once the Newark Housing Authority's redevelopment program attains reality and 46 acres of slum and blighted buildings are torn down to make way for construction of both public and private housing. . . . Eighth Avenue, main artery of the Italian-American community there, will disappear along with its restaurants, bakeries, groceries, and sea food places that attract a large clientele, not only from the neighborhood but from other parts of the city and the suburbs. Also to disappear are the many clubs, political and social, interspersed through the crowded area. Members congregate at these places—most of them converted stores—to play card games and to use the bocci alleys.

Newark News 1/21/1952

Children playing near open fire hydrant in Aqueduct Alley, circa 1952. (Photo: Rebuilding Newark, 1952, Newark Housing Authority)

Demolition of a tract in the First Ward along Seventh Avenue. (Photo: Ace Alagna)

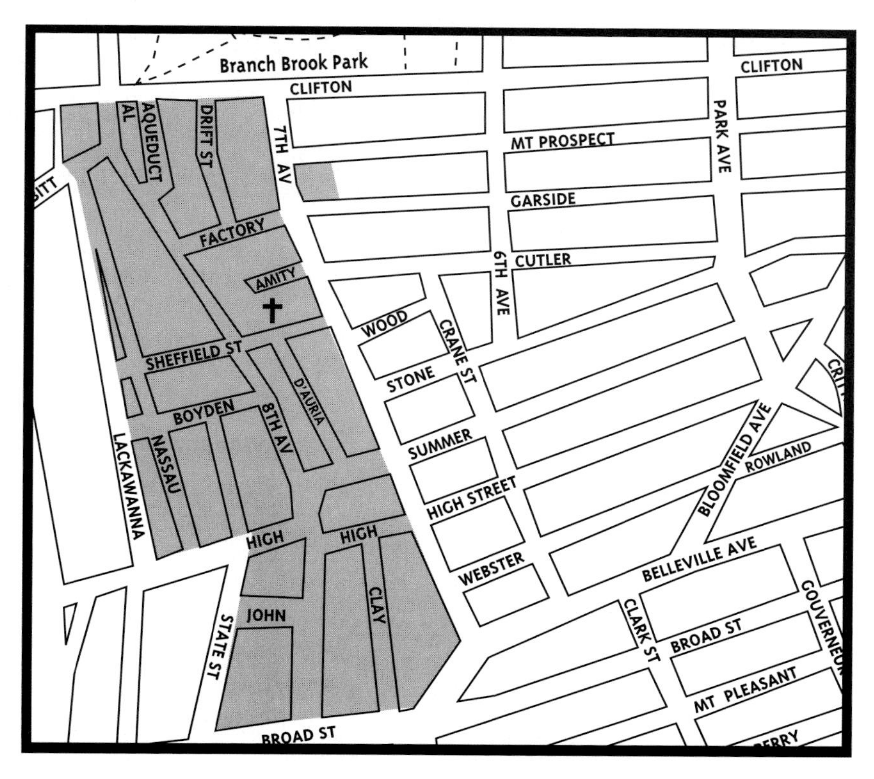

First Ward Italian Quarter

LITTLE ITALY DISTRICT DISPLACED BY URBAN RENEWAL IS SHADED

Clearing the site for Columbus Homes Housing Project in 1953.
(Photo: *Construction Report,* 1956 Newark Housing Authority)

> The Ward has contributed greatly to the history of Newark. The area is complete with its Italian tradition. Visitors are impressed by "Little Italy," and the neighborhood is crowded on Sunday when visitors arrive to buy Italian groceries and other delicacies. But outside of all this local color the housing conditions are terrible. Many homes have no bathtubs, hot water, or toilets. The houses are old and to a large extent are firetraps. The best thing that could have possibly happened is the redevelopment of the entire area.
>
> *Italian Tribune* 1/25/1952

Procession during Feast of Saint Gerard, circa 1960, with Columbus Homes in the background.
(Photo: Saint Lucy's Archives)

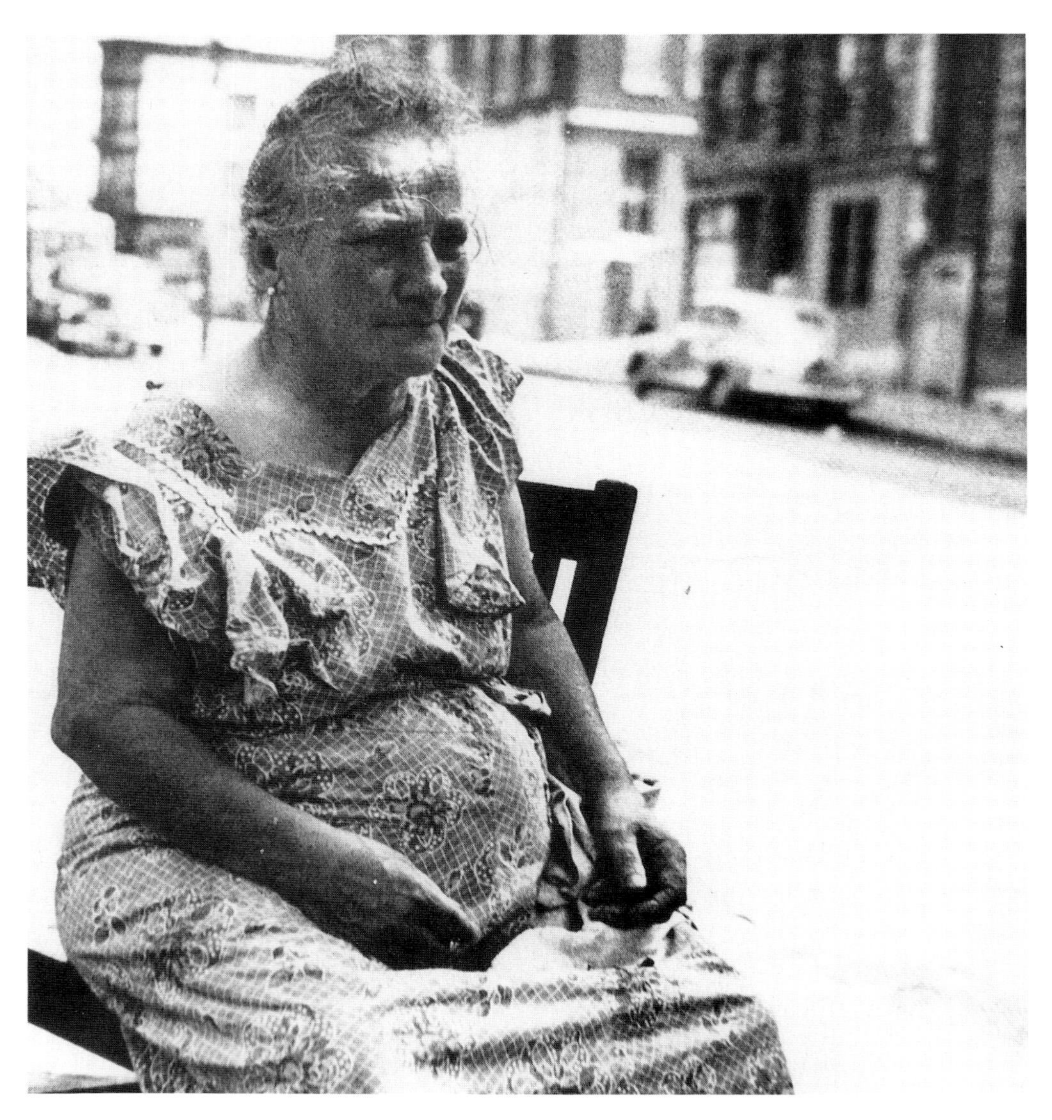

Gelsomina Nicastro, matriarch of the Nicastro family, photographed in 1953 outside her home at 14 Factory Street, on the corner of Drift Street. Twenty-two members of the Nicastro family lived there. It was one of the last buildings to be torn down by urban renewal and some family members remained there almost until the day it came down. The house was leveled in January 1956 and replaced with a parking lot for the Colonnade apartment complex. Drift Street disappeared entirely. Even at the end, a few defiant First Warders refused to leave their homes. When the water was turned off, they drew water from the hydrants. (Photo: Dolores Nicastro)

FAITH AND MEMORY

The Italian First Ward has vanished; nonetheless, First Warders' loyalty and attachment to their old neighborhood and their "sense of place" remains as powerful as ever. Several factors seem to account for this.

The First Ward was a prototype of America's urban ethnic enclaves as they existed during the first half of the twentieth century. Urban neighborhoods engendered a spirit of cohesion and community. The urban neighborhood was a place where the public and the private space intersected in a unique way, producing a kind of social intimacy that animated the neighborhood and forged lasting ties among its inhabitants on a variety of levels.

Life in the neighborhood was multilayered. Each layer—the family, the neighbors, the building, the block, the parish—was woven into a somewhat larger layer. Italian neighborhoods, modeled after the Italian paese, had an additional layer of extended and interlocking families, creating a kind of supra-family that promoted respect for neighbors and reinforced the underlying feeling of connection. "In the First Ward, we were all one big family," recalled Mary Averna. "Everyone was *comare* and *compare,* and that meant you had to bring respect." Mary's father owned a fish market on Sheffield Street before to the Depression, and she was known as Mary Fish until the day she died. "We never kept our doors locked," said Fanny De Donna, whose family owned the Vesuvius Restaurant on

Eighth Avenue. "My father and mother would go to the center market on Mulberry Street at 2 a.m. to shop for the restaurant and return after 4 a.m. Sometimes the bells at Saint Lucy's would be ringing for the first Mass. It didn't matter. We always felt safe." Anthony Coppola, a parishioner at Saint Lucy's Church for more than sixty years and a member of its Guard of Honor, asserted, "We were a community of respect. The whole neighborhood was like a family."

"The First Ward, that's the Italian Shangri La and Brigadoon," said Steve Adubato, Sr., director of the North Ward Educational and Cultural Center, a community-based organization he founded in the early 1970s when the Italian population became more heavily concentrated north of Bloomfield Avenue. Adubato's father directed the Eighth Avenue Boys Club. He likens the First Ward to the Camelot myth, an urban Brigadoon frozen in memory, viewed through the lens of nostalgia. "It was a fantasy place. It was perfect, if life could be perfect. It was one culture. There was a tremendous desire to live in harmony. It is impossible to explain to anyone today what that feeling was. It couldn't exist today."

The neighborhood, First Warders insist, was a place of camaraderie, of respect, and of genuine affection. "It was beautiful," said one. "I was never happier than in those days. Everybody knew everyone. There was no animosity. Just beautiful people." "The neighborhood had tremendous heart," said another. "No matter where you went in the First Ward, there was love and affection." Nostalgia, and a longing for this communal spirit, helps to explain why First Warders state with such conviction, "I'd trade everything today and go back to live there if it could be the way it was then."

The experience of loss and longing for the vanished neighborhood created a First Ward diaspora. The sense of displacement was felt most keenly by those who were forced to leave their homes. But even First Warders who were not initially uprooted by urban renewal are affected by this legacy of being displaced from the neighborhood; it affects those who were barely old enough to recall it, those who left later, and even the grandchildren of those who lived through it. The memory of this experience, which First Warders share with other neighborhood dwellers displaced by urban renewal, such as Boston's West Enders, has not dissipated with time. Even though urban renewal and its aftermath virtually obliterated every trace of the First Ward that had been built by their immigrant parents and grandparents, displaced First Warders never entirely abandoned their old neighborhood.

The venerable Saint Lucy's Church and the annual Feast of Saint Gerard provide this displaced community with a space to which they can return, where the present and the past coexist against the backdrop of a living tradition. It might have been otherwise. Monsignor Granato, pastor of Saint Lucy's Church and its far-flung diaspora, recalls that during the 1970s, at the lowest point in the parish's history, the priests made an unspoken pact with the people of the parish, "If you stay, we stay." He is quick to add, "We all did." Even those who moved far away remained spiritually close to Saint Lucy's. The parish slowly rebounded. Baptisms and attendance at mass increased during the 1980s when the parish built the Villa Vittoria housing complex on Seventh Avenue where elderly parishioners continue to reside.

In 1991 Saint Lucy's parish celebrated its centennial. Three years later the city of Newark began demolition of the long-vacant Columbus Homes. The parish had been campaigning since 1973 to tear down the deteriorated buildings and replace them with low-rise townhouses and garden apartments. It took more than two decades to bring this about, and hundreds of former residents were on hand to witness the first buildings coming down. When a videotape of the demolition was shown a week later at Saint Lucy's Community Center, a visibly moved Monsignor Granato told five hundred applauding parishioners: "Despite everything, you have remained loyal." Granato attributes the "fierce loyalty" of First Warders to the fact that "they didn't walk away from their neighborhood, they were thrown out." Still, they clung to their church. "It was their one bastion," he explains. "It was all that was left."

This loyalty remains undiminished because First Warders are faithful to the traditions celebrated at Saint Lucy's Church, which connect them to family and ancestors who once inhabited the neighborhood. For First Ward Italians, the interior of Saint Lucy's Church is a space like no other in the world. It is more than a sacred space; it is the place where the past can be rekindled. The memory of loved ones and the past which they inhabited is most intensely felt inside the church. People bring their children to Saint Lucy's for baptism because they feel the presence there of parents and grandparents. To many, it feels like coming home.

This sense of a sacred and familial space extends to the streets surrounding Saint Lucy's Church during the annual Feast of Saint Gerard, when those who return to the First Ward literally walk in the footsteps of their grandparents. Mothers bring children, especially the newborn, for the priests to bless with the relic of Saint Gerard, just as their parents had before them. Many First Warders will contend that the first time they marched with the saint was when they were carried in their mothers' wombs.

In 1977 the Catholic Conference of Bishops designated Saint Lucy's the National Shrine of Saint Gerard, and each year many come to the feast on chartered buses from out of state. Not surprisingly, the devotion to Saint Gerard at Saint Lucy's Church has grown with the passage of time. Thousands overflow the church for each of the several masses on the saint's feast day. During the processions, elaborate capes with dollar bills are still affixed to the statue as it weaves its way through the streets, accompanied by the band playing. Few would dispute the fact that the feast sustains the church. The church, in turn, provides the unbroken link with the past, with the vanished neighborhood.

Only the church remains. Timeless and changeless. And within the confines of the church, as one recognizes a familiar face, albeit age-worn and wizened, it is easy for a moment to let the intervening years fade from memory and to imagine the old neighborhood still thriving and alive outside the church doors, the boisterous sounds, the exuberant feasts, the rag-tag bands, and the smell of bakeries, the peddlers and the pushcarts, U Fumo and Fatigado, the voices of countless friends, and the smile of a beloved grandparent . . . the old First Ward, the way it once was.

Implosion of Columbus Homes, March 6, 1994. As early as 1973 the Columbus Homes were in such terrible shape that comparisons were being drawn to the Pruitt-Igo complex in Saint Louis, which that year became the first housing development to be razed. Newark's housing was rated the worst in the country that year. (Photo: New Jersey Newsphotos)

Saint Gerard Feast at Saint Lucy's Church in 1994. (Photo: *Italian Tribune*)

ABOUT THE AUTHOR

Michael Immerso is a writer, publicist, and social activist. A graduate of Rutgers University's Newark College of Arts and Sciences (1973), he was a prominent student leader and community activist. He subsequently published a community newspaper in Newark's predominantly Italian North Ward. Throughout the 1980s, he was active, both locally and nationally, as a leader of the nuclear freeze movement and frequently serves as a media consultant for nonprofit organizations. In 1994 he established the First Ward Documentary Project, and in 1996, he was curator for the Newark Public Library's exhibition which inaugurated the collection. He is a life-long resident of Newark, whose great-grandparents settled in the First Ward in the 1890s.